Praise for *Branch Rickey* by Jimmy Breslin

"So many unforgettably d[...] Breslin's wonderful new B[...] seemingly threaten to bu[...] The Rickey-Robinson stor[...] as colorfully or entertainingly as it is by Breslin. . . . You might read a longer baseball book this year, but you won't read a better one."　　　　　　　　　　 —*Sports Illustrated*

"What Breslin has done, with his usual gritty perception, is revive a story of enormous consequence. . . . [He] is a master of the spare narrative."　　　　　　 —*The New York Times*

"In just 146 pages Breslin brilliantly explains how and why [Rickey] changed baseball and the United States for the better. . . . An excellent book. Go get it and read it."
　　　　　　　　　　　　　　 —*San Jose Mercury News*

"You'll want to wedge a copy of *Branch Rickey* in your gym bag. . . . This new biography by legendary newspaper columnist Jimmy Breslin is peppery, original, opinionated, and irresistible. . . . A seriously entertaining book."
　　　　　　　　　　　　　　　　 —*Chicago Tribune*

"[Breslin] is as old-school as they come, both as a writer and as a baseball fan. So it's not surprising that his terse new biography of Branch Rickey, part of the Penguin Lives series, is punchy, and anecdote- and attitude-driven. . . . His cigar-chomping style and flair for capturing the world of baseball as Rickey was transforming it makes for brisk reading."　　　　　　　 —*Milwaukee Journal Sentinel*

"Breslin brings his trademark grit and grace to the combustible issue of civil rights in baseball."
　　　　　　　　　　　　　　　　 —*The Washington Post*

"Numerous biographies of Branch Rickey have been written over the years. Several of them are very good, but none is quite like Jimmy Breslin's spirited and idiosyncratic little book. . . . An old-time newspaper man, Breslin has a flair for blunt prose with a dash of wit. . . . The result is a lively portrait of a man the author refers to as a 'Great American' that is informative and highly entertaining."

—*The Christian Science Monitor*

"[Rickey] was a giant of the game when the game was still the most powerful and important sport in the nation, and Breslin's rat-a-tat-tat sportswriter's voice is perfect for chronicling that scene; you can almost hear the typewriter keys clacking." —*The Boston Globe*

A LIPPER™ / PENGUIN BOOK

BRANCH RICKEY

Jimmy Breslin was born in Jamaica, Queens. He is the author of multiple bestselling and critically acclaimed books, and was awarded the 1986 Pulitzer Prize for distinguished commentary. He lives in New York City.

JIMMY BRESLIN

Branch Rickey

A LIFE

A LIPPER™ / PENGUIN BOOK

PENGUIN BOOKS

Published by the Penguin Group

Penguin Group (USA) Inc., 375 Hudson Street, New York, New York 10014, U.S.A.
Penguin Group (Canada), 90 Eglinton Avenue East, Suite 700, Toronto,
Ontario, Canada M4P 2Y3 (a division of Pearson Penguin Canada Inc.)
Penguin Books Ltd, 80 Strand, London WC2R 0RL, England
Penguin Ireland, 25 St Stephen's Green, Dublin 2, Ireland
(a division of Penguin Books Ltd)
Penguin Books Australia Ltd, 250 Camberwell Road, Camberwell,
Victoria 3124, Australia (a division of Pearson Australia Group Pty Ltd)
Penguin Books India Pvt Ltd, 11 Community Centre,
Panchsheel Park, New Delhi–110 017, India
Penguin Group (NZ), 67 Apollo Drive, Rosedale, Auckland 0632,
New Zealand (a division of Pearson New Zealand Ltd)
Penguin Books (South Africa) (Pty) Ltd, 24 Sturdee Avenue,
Rosebank, Johannesburg 2196, South Africa

Penguin Books Ltd, Registered Offices: 80 Strand, London WC2R 0RL, England

First published in the United States of America by Viking Penguin,
a member of Penguin Group (USA) Inc. 2011
Published in Penguin Books 2012

3 5 7 9 10 8 6 4 2

Copyright © Jimmy Breslin, 2011
All rights reserved

THE LIBRARY OF CONGRESS HAS CATALOGED THE HARDCOVER EDITION AS FOLLOWS:
Breslin, Jimmy.
Branch Rickey / Jimmy Breslin.
p. cm.—(A penguin life)
Includes bibliographical references and index.
ISBN 978-0-670-02249-6 (hc.)
ISBN 978-0-14-312047-6 (pbk.)
1. Rickey, Branch, 1881–1965.   2. Baseball team owners—United States—Biography.
3. Brooklyn Dodgers (Baseball team)—Presidents—Biography.   I. Title.
GV865.R45B74 2010
796.357092—dc22
[B]   2010035008
Printed in the United States of America

Set in Centennial LT Std 45 Light
Designed by Francesca Belanger

For Charles V. Feeney, aka Pally

Branch Rickey

PROLOGUE

Beautiful. When they ask me to write a book about a Great American, right away I say yes. When I say yes I always mean no. They ask me to choose a subject, and I say Branch Rickey. He placed the first black baseball player into the major leagues. His name was Jackie Robinson. He helped clear the sidewalks for Barack Obama to come into the White House. As it only happened once in the whole history of the country, I would say that is pretty good. Then some editors told me they never heard of Rickey. Which I took as an insult, a disdain for what I know, as if it is not important enough for them to bother with.

So now I had to write the book.

Simultaneously, I had a problem for a writer as bad as sprained hands. The rule I followed from my first day as a copyboy in the sports departments was that you couldn't write about a game unless you went to see it. These people who tried reporting by watching television were killing readers with lifeless stories. It still is like this, except there are many fewer readers to murder.

The trouble is, I spoke to Branch Rickey only once in my whole life. I am with my friend Rusty Wilde at Ebbets Field, where maybe two hundred spectators sit in a big rainstorm watching the Brooklyn Dodgers football team play against the Chicago Rockets. I was a copyboy after school at the old *Long Island Press* and got the tickets from the sports department. The newspaper is gone as are both teams.

Into the seat behind me comes Rickey, the Dodgers owner, in a yellow slicker, with lackeys to the left and right. He says, "Hello, boys." I am on my high school football team and must show how much I know. I ask him why his star quarterback is playing what was known as a single wing formation. They start each play by passing a wet ball back to him, and in all this mud you can't handle the ball so good.

"He ought to be in a T," I say. "We got the best T quarterback ever to live from around here."

Rickey says, "Who is that?"

I say, "Sidney Luckman."

Rickey says, "I've heard of him." He was playing me for a fool. Luckman was already a legend.

I say, "He comes out of Erasmus Hall High. At Flatbush and Church. My uncle took me to see him play Lincoln, down by Coney Island." I was as smart as they come. Rickey now ignores me and I don't pick up half of what I could have. I wanted to go back to the sports department at the school newspaper and show off with what I heard him say. When I did overhear him, I concentrated totally on every word. I hunched over and wrote a couple of key words on a sheet of copypaper that was folded in three. That was the way the big reporters did it. The paper was cheap city room newsprint. I wrote "concept of education?" and "leading characteristic match their ability." If I had paid attention like this in school I would have had a full scholarship to Oxford.

I never saw Branch Rickey again and now I am going to write a great book about him. I was sure I had a lifesaver. Jack Lang, whom I know for maybe fifty years, has been writing newspaper stories about Rickey for a long time. I am going to see him next week. Then I am in the shower and my wife hollers, "Jack Lang died." I said a prayer. After a period of mourning, I started again. I called Emil "Buzzie" Bavasi at his home in San Diego. He was an assistant to Rickey and was in the room when they decided to bring up Jackie Robinson. "Come out and we'll go over the whole thing," he said. Two days later I pick up the paper and read that Buzzie died.

I figured I would be able to rely on big-name historians whom I have yet to read and that this would be immensely pleasurable. And then I read the books. History writers should be put not in the jail but under it.

The only books on the subject you can tolerate are *Branch Rickey: American in Action*, by Arthur Mann; *Branch Rickey: Baseball's Ferocious Gentleman*, by Lee Lowenfish; *First Class Citizenship: The Civil Rights Letters of Jackie Robinson*, edited by Michael Long; *Branch Rickey*, by Murray Polner; *Jackie Robinson*, by Arnold Rampersad; *Baseball's Great Experiment: Jackie Robinson and His Legacy*, by Jules Tygiel; and *Notes on Duels and Duelling*, by Lorenzo Sabine. As you read them, you become exhausted realizing the work these men have done. Polner is a friend, but I would save and reread his work even if I hated him.

In addition to reading, I used my two legs, which always have taken me through confusing jobs. Walk the streets, find old addresses, climb stairs, go to a nursing home or a saloon. Find somebody whose grandfather was there. Listen.

I also bring to this book, readers all, a full love of topic, plus humor and skepticism. Herewith, a look at the life and times and accomplishments of Branch Rickey.

CHAPTER ONE

This is a January morning in 1943 and Wesley Branch Rickey is standing outside his house at 34 Greenway South in Forest Hills Gardens, Queens, New York City. At age sixty-one, his hair remains thick and dark. His eyebrows jut like rocky ledges, like something from an old photo of John L. Lewis, the labor leader. Rickey's face shows eagerness and excitement even after all his years in baseball. He has asked God for help and believes that is exactly what is happening now.

Delightful chimes only Rickey can hear come from high in the sky, sounding softly and clearly through the bare limbs of the trees lining the street. He waits in cold, fresh air for his ride to downtown Brooklyn, where he runs the Dodgers baseball team. While this does not sound so vital, especially in time of war, today he is doing the work of the Lord with all his heart and mind and these large, gnarled hands he waves. He is going to a crucial meeting with the banker who holds the mortgage on the Dodgers baseball team.

Rickey carries with him a Midwestern Christian religious fervor as strong as a wheat crop, and a political faith in anything Republican. Already he is a familiar figure at his new church in Queens, the Church in the Gardens, only steps down the narrow street from his house. It is a place of worship as lovely as it sounds, built with stone from Europe. On Sundays, Branch Rickey brought with him to church a prayer book and a background of Methodist studies from Ohio Wesleyan University, and sometimes he delivered the sermon. In one, he announced he was here to run the Brooklyn Dodgers and to serve the God to whom they prayed, and the Lord's work called for him to bring the first black player into major league baseball.

You held the American heart in your hand when you attempted to change anything in baseball. If a black was involved, the cardiograms showed an ice storm.

Baseball was a sport for hillbillies with great eyesight. Rickey read books and as a young man was the catcher in town games and made it to the big leagues, but only for a very short time. He never went to high school, but his first job was as a schoolteacher. Later he taught college freshman English, Latin, Shakespeare, and Greek drama, and read for the law in his free time. Sometimes, in directing his players, he mixes all these things together. Then he brings it down to their level in a drill for pitchers by putting a twenty-dollar bill atop a hat on home plate and telling them to hit it.

Rickey is here just a few months from St. Louis, where he put together the Cardinals teams that won six National League pennants and four World Series, one of them just last fall against the Yankees. The only thing he couldn't do in St. Louis was move black fans out of the broiling one-hundred-degree sun of the bleachers and into the shaded grandstand. When Rickey asked the Cardinals' owner Sam

Breadon to get rid of the segregated-seating rule, Breadon, from Greenwich Village in Manhattan, knew Rickey was right, but not as right as the gasoline that people in that near-Southern city would splash over the wooden stands in order to burn them to the ground. "Business is business," he told Rickey, turning him down.

In no calling, craft, profession, trade, or occupation was color in America accepted. The annals of the purported greats show that everyone was paralyzed with the national disease: color fear.

But here on this street corner stands Branch Rickey, a lone white man with a fierce belief that it is the deepest sin against God to hold color against a person. On this day he means to change baseball and America, too. The National Pastime, the game that teaches sportsmanship to children, must shake with shame, Rickey thought. Until this morning in Forest Hills, there has been no white person willing to take on the issue. That is fine with Rickey. He feels that he is at bat with two outs and a 3-2 pitch coming. He is the last man up, sure he will get a hit.

At 7:00 a.m. on this same morning, George V. McLaughlin leaves his duplex at 35 Prospect Park West, Brooklyn. The great park lawns across the street brittle with frost. He still hasn't the slightest idea of what beyond team finances Branch Rickey wants to discuss. Right away there is the pealing of bells from St. Saviour's Catholic Church nearby. They ring for what he would accomplish on this day.

McLaughlin had climbed a ladder of religion, politics, and hard work. His father was a ferryboat captain and

young McLaughlin's schooling in Brooklyn stressed showing up on time for work. One of his early jobs was at a bank
and simultaneously he got a degree at night from New York
University. Then he went to law school and taught account-
ing after hours before becoming a lawyer, police commissioner, state banking superintendent, and now president
of the Brooklyn Trust Company, to which the Dodgers owe
$800,000. He wants to get paid.

McLaughlin and Rickey were raised to call to God from
under different roofs. Rickey was a proclaimed Methodist,
devout conservative, and Prohibitionist. George V. McLaughlin had heard of people other than Roman Catholics but
couldn't tell you if he had met many. His temporal belief consisted of the Brooklyn Democratic Party. He said that anyone
in Brooklyn who didn't vote for Franklin D. Roosevelt should
be committed. McLaughlin was called "George the Fifth" because he was in charge wherever he went and if he took a
drink of Scotch that was none of your business.

Rickey is from the hills and swamps of southern Ohio,
and was raised singing Methodist hymns in a wagon going
to church on Sunday. Wesley Branch Rickey was named
after John Wesley, who founded Methodism in England in
1739, a precept of which was "Think and let think." The
scriptures mention a "branch" that helped make Wesley a
saint. Rickey's religion and politics were inseparable, and
made it only natural for him to campaign for the Eighteenth
Amendment, which was Prohibition. Get out there and
break all those whiskey bottles that cause men and, yes,
women, too, to become filthy pigs and wallow in the worst
of sins. He finally stopped supporting the amendment but

only because it didn't work. He told the Brooklyn Rotary Club, "The cause of prohibition, a most worthy one, was thrown back a hundred years by the Volstead Act."

Even in a ballpark where everybody but the third baseman drank big cold beers, Rickey remains openly against drink. There is the night when sportswriter Arch Murray of the *New York Post* sees Rickey in a box at Forbes Field in Pittsburgh and runs through the stands to get to him. Every day of his life, Arch wears a Princeton tie in honor of his old school and conducts a one-person tailgate party. His breath requires corking. Rickey inhales once in his presence and immediately begins talking vigorously, waving his hands. Arch nods and listens intently. Seeing this, the other reporters become anxious, saying, look, Rickey is giving Arch an exclusive. Arch returns from his private audience muttering, "He's right. He's right. He's right."

"What is he right about?" someone asks.

"I should stop drinking."

So here this morning is Rickey, a man of total abstinence and an active member of the St. Louis Grace Methodist Episcopal Church, with strong ties to the St. Louis City Evangelical Union, taking his dreams to a Brooklyn banker. This man, Rickey thinks, doesn't agree with me on everything. Still, Rickey is sure where George V. would be in a decent fight. George V. had a great aversion to moving backward. You could find him at lunch each day in Room 40 of the Bossert Hotel, where anybody who was a name in Brooklyn business or politics came to show respect. When George V. raised a thumb on your behalf, you had unbeatable support.

At the Brooklyn Trust Company, McLaughlin had in his hands the accounts of the large pharmaceutical company started by Charles Pfizer, and sprawling real estate empires and construction companies, too. As the head of the financially creaky Dodgers baseball team, McLaughlin walked through a world of smiles, claps on the back, and congratulations. If you were prominent enough, you could get players' autographs from George V. and become a towering figure with your kids. In his Brooklyn, only rosary beads blessed by the Pope could mean more.

For the meeting with McLaughlin, Rickey arrived on crowded Court Street, which sloped down to the East River and the big, brawling Brooklyn Navy Yard, source of thousands of warships with crews as white as their uniforms. Rickey and George McLaughlin held their meeting four years before the armed forces were desegregated by Harry Truman, years before *Brown v. Board*, decades before the Civil Rights Act and the great American law, Lyndon Baines Johnson's Voting Rights Act of 1965 (and that is exactly how it should be printed in the books). On this day Martin Luther King, Jr., was a junior at an Atlanta high school.

McLaughlin was not famous for working with or socializing with blacks. This was no surprise to Rickey, and so he looked right past it to find any strength that could get him home. Usually he judged a man's ability to hit behind the runner; this time he was measuring a guy at a desk. Going in, his scouting report on McLaughlin was brief: a crackerjack. Where is he on civil rights for blacks? It doesn't matter where he is when it starts. Look for where he'll be at the finish.

Rickey figured it would be best to let McLaughlin extol Democrats while he listened avidly. Keep low opinion of Roosevelt out of the conversation, he warned himself. At some point in the business talk, Rickey mentioned to McLaughlin that he wanted to make a large expenditure for scouts. These men would find good players who were too young to be drafted into the war now but would serve someday soon, and then, God willing, come home strong and swift and eager to play. Some of the prospects now were as young as fifteen and sixteen; there was this boy in Compton, California, everybody called him Duke, last name Snider. Rickey's plan would bring all that young talent to play alongside returning Brooklyn veterans. McLaughlin was in favor.

"By the way, all these scouts would cost a lot of money," Rickey said.

McLaughlin still loved the idea. "We'll get a march on all of them."

Rickey now made a careful choice of his words and tone. Be passionate. No, entirely inappropriate. Be nonchalant. Not that, either. Why not just try the truth? This is no coward we have here. This is a secure man. So he told McLaughlin that by looking for all this new talent, the scouts might come across "a Negro player or two."

McLaughlin showed nothing. Of course he knew exactly what this meant. Rickey was not just throwing out a casual idea. The man would bring a stranger under the roof, a black who should be mowing lawns and instead would be running bases in this white national sport.

Then George V. started to count.

His friend Bill Shea remembered: "He figured that at the least there were a million blacks who played baseball. He knew right there in that room that it was only sensible to look for players who could make the Dodgers. And fill seats at Ebbets Field and all over the league. The players who could do it were out there."

McLaughlin had an old style of reasoning that came from years in police stations and bank negotiations. "If you want to do this to get a beat on the other teams and make some money, then let's do it," he told Rickey. "But if you want to do this for some social change, forget it. We want to win and make money. Don't try to bring principle into this. If this doesn't work for money, you're sunk."

Rickey tingled inside. He had found a man whose seemingly flat indifference to the enormity of the subject, reducing it from a religious calling to a way of making more money, gave hope. What these two men had just done was agree to put their hands into the troubled history of America and fix it, starting in a baseball dugout.

As they were now partners in this undertaking, Rickey asked McLaughlin to get the other directors together and clear this sudden and large scouting expenditure. McLaughlin said sure, why not? He put together a luncheon with George Barnewall, a close friend of McLaughlin's at the Brooklyn Trust, Joe Gilleaudeau, who represented the Ebbets family, and James Mulvey of the McKeever interest.

The luncheon was at the New York Athletic Club, on the corner of Central Park South and Seventh Avenue in Manhattan. McLaughlin said that if they had tried to meet in

12

Brooklyn, the first fifty people seeing them would spy or hound the subject out of them. The AC, as it was known whenever decent Catholics gathered, was an unlikely site to introduce a black into anything; the club didn't even have one caring for the garbage. Sportswriters who might be hanging around the club would be easy to shoo away. McLaughlin knew what to do if any Catholics might wander by: Give a look that said, "I'll have you in detention pens." And there would be no Jewish sportswriters disturbing the secrecy because there were no Jews allowed inside the club, either. Once, Norton Peppis, the great Queens gambler, was pursued by Ruby Stein, a racket guy who wanted his money, right up to the doorway of the AC, which Peppis, with a smattering of Irish blood, jumped through while Stein stood on the sidewalk and caterwauled about anti-Semitism.

At the meeting, George V. McLaughlin opened the conversation by saying he thought that Rickey had a great idea about scouting that could mean blacks would be signed to play for the team. Because it was George V. saying this, nobody choked, as they might have if anybody else was talking. McLaughlin lectured the table that this was about the greatest virtue, making money. Barnewell said, "We probably haven't tapped the Negro market enough." The others agreed.

I am playing with children, Rickey thought. George V. then turned it over to Rickey, whose bushy eyebrows were bunched. His voice was low and rolled on without pause. The cigar in his right hand provided the smoke and his waving left hand was the mirror.

13

"Prejudice," Rickey told the table. "It reflects an attitude of a great many people in this country who don't introspect themselves very closely about their own prejudices. . . . You can't meet it with words. You can't take prejudice straight on. It must be done by proximity. Proximity! The player alongside you. No matter what the skin color or language. Win the game. Win all. Get the championship and the check that goes with it."

Rickey and McLaughlin were probably the only men in the room who actually worked for a living. How do we handle these owners if they oppose us, McLaughlin remembered thinking.

On the way back to his Montague Street office, Rickey had the driver stop at Ebbets Field, the home of the Dodgers. A watchman let him in and he went past the closed hot dog and beer stand and out to the seats behind home plate. He still was new and had never before noticed the sign running along the bottom of the scoreboard on the right field fence. It was a delight to Brooklyn fans. The sign was knee high and it called out the hallowed name of the clothing store owned by Abe Stark. In the bottom left and bottom right corners of the long sign, inside circles, was a message: "Hit Sign Win Suit." Only a freak low line drive would put Abe's threads on you.

Rickey was delighted by the sign. There was also a big, bold ad for whiskey: "Schenley's. That's All." Rickey imagined this sign being ripped down and scrubbed away and the space sold to some decent business that believed in fighting sin. He also wanted a ban on beer at the ballpark. He would let the fans face summer heat with only vile Coca-Cola as a defense.

Staring at the infield in empty Ebbets Field, Rickey suddenly saw in the gray winter afternoon a player tearing past second on the way to third. The player's short sleeves were whipping in the wind. Little clumps of dirt shot up from his spikes.

Now Rickey saw the unfamiliar figure dancing down the line from third. His head threatened a race for the plate, the most exciting play of all, stealing home. He was rocking joyously off the base and ready to explode with the pitch.

When it comes, the catcher leaps as if electricity has hit him. He is ready to fire to third. The runner goes back to the base.

Now the pitcher is ready again. He has his leg coming up and his arm in a windup, and down the third base line comes the runner. Running furiously. Good Lord, is he going all the way?

No. He stops dead, halfway down the line.

Rickey is so excited that he is talking to himself.

"Why is the pitcher winding up?" he asks. "Why doesn't he just stretch and hold the runner on? Good Lord, he is making it easy. Oh, see. Here it is this time."

It is. The pitcher has a long, complicated windup and here comes the runner, powerful legs flying, head down. *Who is he?* thinks Rickey. I can't see his face with his cap pulled down. He slides. His feet flash under the tag.

He steals home!

The player rises up with his back to Rickey. He lopes into the grayness. As he disappears, Rickey gets a fleeting glance at a dark-skinned face.

Soon, Rickey is excitedly sending his scouts out searching for this base runner, this black man, whom they had never sought before except while hailing parking lot attendants. He was out there somewhere in the mists and he would be found. At that moment he was a dream figure who only Rickey could see, somebody with no name or face or features other than dark skin, a man not yet visible but already a destiny.

CHAPTER TWO

That mysterious player who stole home in front of Rickey at Ebbets Field was nearly lost forever to the thing he was supposed to change, American racism. His name was Jack Roosevelt Robinson, and to look at what happened to him, as a soldier in the United States Army with the rank of lieutenant, is to see how much had to be overcome.

Robinson was arrested on July 17, 1944, at the McCloskey hospital in Temple, Texas, on the outskirts of Fort Hood. Rickey's dream for changing the nation sat in a bare courtroom at Fort Hood that August with multiple charges against him in a general court-martial. It all came about due to a dispute over a seat on a bus that was outside army jurisdiction, and so most of the charges were thrown out. But two remained. One was conduct unbecoming an officer, which could mean anything. The other had to do with refusal to obey an order during time of war, and the circumstances may seem innocuous—Jackie didn't stay in a room when he was ordered to—but it was ominous at the time. In a court of nine officers, several of whom had been in combat and understood the gravity of the charge, he faced a possible long sentence. Any hope for a career would be gone.

STATEMENT of Mr. Milton N. Renegar, Bus Driver, Southwestern Bus Company, 7 July 1944:

I drive a bus for the Southwestern Bus Company. At approximately 10:15, 6 July 1944, I was driving my bus and stopped at Bus Stop #23, on 172nd Street, Camp Hood, Texas. Some white ladies, maybe a soldier or so, and a colored girl and a colored Second Lieutenant got on the bus. The colored girl and the colored Lt., whom I later learned to be 2nd Lt. Jack R. Robinson of the 761st Tank Battalion, sat down together about middle ways of the bus. On that particular run I have quite a few of the white ladies who work in the PX's and ride the bus at that hour almost every night. I did not say anything to the colored Lt. when he first sat down, until I got around to Bus Stop #18, and then I asked him, I said, "Lt., if you don't mind, I have got several ladies to pick up at this Stop and will have a load of them before I get back to the Central Bus Station, and would like for you to move back to the rear of the bus if you don't mind." When I asked him to move back to the rear he just sat there, and I asked him to move back there a second time. When I asked him the second time he started cursing and the first thing he said was, "I'm not going to move a God dammed bit." I told him that I had a load of ladies to pick up and that I was sure they wouldn't want to ride mixed up like that, and told him I'd rather he would either move back to the rear or get off the bus, one of the two. He kept on cursing and saying he wasn't going to get back, and I told him that he could either get back or he'd be sorry of it when I got to the Bus Station, or words to that effect. He kept saying something about it after I started up the bus, but I could not understand what he was saying. He continued to sit there with the colored girl and the girl did not say anything. When we arrived at the Bus Station I had "Pinky" Younger, the Dispatcher, call the MP's. Everybody on the bus was mad about it. I had asked the Lt. in a nice way to move and he had refused. One of the ladies who was riding said, "I don't mind waiting on them all day, but when I get on the bus at night to go home, I'm not about to ride all mixed up with them."

This lady works at PX #10 and I believe her daughter works with her and was with her last night. The colored Lt. kept on doing a lot of cursing and the feeling on the bus was pretty bad. All the people were very much upset about the situation and wanted something done about the Lieutenant's attitude. When I told the Dispatcher to call the MP's I told him I was having some trouble with a negro Lieutenant. This white lady asked me if I was going to report the Lieutenant and I told her, "Yes," and she said, "Well, if you don't I am." At that time the colored Lieutenant said to the lady, "You better quit fuckin' with me," and he meant everybody that was trying to do something about the trouble he was causing. There were white women and children and soldiers present, it looked to me like forty or fifty people within hearing distance, and when the Lt. said that, it was outside the Bus Station but could have been heard plainly inside the Station. After the MP's arrived and the Lt. went to get in the patrol wagon he called me a "son-of-a-bitch," and walked around to get in the wagon, he said, "I don't know why the son-of-a-bitch wanted to give me all this trouble," and the women were all still there at that time. The MP's just asked the Lt. a few questions and he kept cursing and so the MP told him he was using a lot of bad language in the presence of ladies and told him he was going to take him over to the Provost Marshal Office and let him talk to the Provost Marshal about it. I told the Lieutenant to hush once and he just kept on raving and cursing. What the Lieutenant said to the lady in the presence of other ladies as I have stated it above, he said three or four other times, and said it to everyone there. He also said something about this white lady as he went around to get in the patrol wagon and I know he was cursing the lady, but I could not tell what he said. I heard him say something to the MP about wanting his name and organization, but I don't know what that was. The only time I heard the colored girl who was with him say anything was when he started to leave with the MP's and she just asked him what the trouble was.

STATEMENT of Mrs. Virginia Jones, 702 Pearl Street, Belton, Texas, 19 July 1944:

I am the wife of 1st Lt. Gordon H. Jones, Jr., 761st Tank Battalion, Camp Hood, Texas. I was with Lt. Jack R. Robinson on the night of 6 July 1944. We left the colored officers club and caught a bus in front of the officers club. I got on the bus first and sat down, and Lt. Robinson got on and came and sat beside me. I sat in the fourth seat from the rear of the bus, which I always considered the rear of the bus. The bus driver told Lt. Robinson to move and Lt. Robinson said, "I'm not moving." The bus driver stopped the bus, came back and balled his fist and said, "Will you move back?" Lt. Robinson said, "I'm not moving," so the bus driver stood there and glared a minute and said, "Well, just sit there until we get down to the bus station."

We got to the bus station and Lt. Robinson and I were the last two to leave the bus. The bus driver detained Lt. Robinson and demanded to see his pass. Lt. Robinson said, "My pass?" and the bus driver said, "Yes, I want to see your pass." Lt. Robinson asked why did he want to see his pass, and then we got off the bus. A woman walked up to Robinson and shook a finger in his face and said, "I'm going to report you because you had a right to move when he asked you to." She stood there and argued with Lt. Robinson awhile, and I don't remember what all was said. Lt. Robinson did not say anything at first and then he said, "Go on and leave me alone." So she walked into the bus station, and about that time the crowd around the bus driver and Lt. Robinson thinned out, and the bus driver said something to the Lt. which I could not hear. No one was close enough to hear, but whatever it was riled Lt. Robinson and he walked up to the bus driver and said something to the bus driver. I did not hear what he said because I wasn't close enough to hear.

STATEMENT of Mrs. Elizabeth Poitevint, Civilian Employee, PX #10, Camp Hood:

When we got to the Central Bus Station we all got

off, and the driver asked the Lieutenant for his identification card, and the Lt. said, "I haven't done anything and I'm not going to show you my identification card, I'm going to get on another bus and go on." The driver said, "I want your identification card to turn you in," then I said to the driver, "If you want any witnesses for what he has done to you, you can call on me, because I've heard everything he has said." Then the Lt. turned to me and said, "Listen here you damned old woman, you have nothing to say about what's going on. I didn't want to get into this, they drafted me into this, and my money is just as good as a white man's." And I told him, I said, "Well, listen buddy, you ought to know where you should sit on a bus." I started on to the bus station and I asked the bus driver if he was going to report him, and I told him that if he didn't report the colored Lt. then I was going to report him to the MP's. I had to wait on them during the day, but I didn't have to sit with them on the bus. . . ."

STATEMENT of General Gerald M. Bear, Captain, Assistant Provost Marshal, Camp Hood, Texas:

Arriving at the MP Guard Room, 2305 on 6 July 1944, I found 2nd Lt. Jack R. Robinson in the MP guard room. I asked the Lt. to step outside the MP Guard Room to wait in the receiving room. Captain Wiggington, Camp OD, was relating and explaining to me what had just occurred as to the incident at the Central Bus Station, Camp Hood, Texas. Lt. Robinson kept continually interrupting Captain Wiggington and myself and kept coming to the guard room door-gate.

I cautioned and requested Lt. Robinson on several different occasions to remain at ease and remain in the receiving room, that I would talk to him later. In an effort to try to be facetious, Lt. Robinson bowed with several sloppy salutes, repeating several times, "OK, sir. OK, sir." on each occasion. I then gave Lt. Robinson a direct order to remain in the receiving room and be seated on a chair, on the far side of the receiving room. Later on I found Lt. Robinson on the outside, talking to the driver of the 761st Tank Battalion OD's jeep. I then directed Lt. Robinson to go inside the building and remain in the receiving room.

Lt. Robinson's attitude in general was disrespectful and impertinent to his superior officers, and very unbecoming to an officer in the presence of enlisted men.

STATEMENT of 2nd Lt. Jack R. Robinson, 0-103158, Company B, 761st Tank Battalion, Camp Hood, Texas, taken in the Military Police Orderly room, Camp Hood, Texas, 0030, 7 July, 1944:

I left McCloskey General Hospital, Temple, Texas, about 1730, 6 July 1944, and went to Temple, Texas on the City Bus. I got on another bus and came out to the Officers Club, Camp Hood, Texas, the colored officers club located on 172nd Street. I arrived there at approximately 1930. I was in the club for some time. While in the club I saw Captain McHenry, Lt. Long, Captain Woodruff and Captain Wales.

I remained in the Officers Club until approximately 2½ hours later. At approximately 2200 I got on the bus at 172nd Street and Battalion, I believe, just outside the colored officers club. I got on the Camp Hood bus. I entered at the front of the bus and moved toward the rear and saw a colored girl sitting in a seat at the middle of the bus. I sat down beside the girl. I knew this girl before. Her name is Mrs. Jones. I don't know her first name. She's an officer's wife here on the post. I sat down there and we rode approximately five or six blocks on the bus and the bus driver turns around and tells me to move to the rear which I do not do. . . . He tells me that if I don't move to the rear he will make trouble for me when we get to the bus station, and I told him if he wanted to make trouble for me that was up to him. When we got to the bus station a lady got off the bus before I got off, and she tells me that she is going to prefer charges against me. That was a white lady. And I said that's all right, too, I don't care if she prefers charges against me. The bus driver asked me for my identification card. I refused to give it to him. He then went to the Dispatcher and told him something. What he told him I don't know. He then comes back and tells the people that this nigger is making trouble. I told the bus driver to stop fuckin with me, so he gets the rest of the men around there and starts blowing his top and someone calls the MP's. Outside of telling this lady that I didn't care if she preferred charges against me or not. I don't know if they were around or not, sir, I was speaking direct to that bus driver, and just as I told the captain (indicating Captain Wigginton, Camp Officer of the Day), if any of you called me a nigger I would do the same thing, especially from a civilian, a general, or anybody else. I mean I would tell them the same thing. I told him I'm just using a "general," any general, if anybody calls me a nigger, I don't know the definition of it. That's just like anyone going around calling you something you don't know what is. The colored girl was going to Belton, her home, and she got off the same time that I got off. The only time I made any statement was when this fellow called me a nigger. I didn't have any loud nor boisterous conversation. That's the only profane language I used if you call it profane. (When told by Captain Bear that that was vulgar and vile language Lt. Robinson said: "That's vulgar is it, that's vile is it?")

I want to tell you right now sir, this private you got out there, he made a statement. The private over in that room. I told him that if he, a private, ever call me a name (a nigger) again I would break him in two.

Robinson had asked the NAACP to get him a lawyer. Instead, the court offered William A. Cline, an officer in a tank outfit who had been assigned to legal affairs. "I come from about as far south as you can go," he told Robinson. The way he said it made him all right with his new client. The trial took four hours. At every break, Robinson ran to the phone and called his fiancée, Rachel, in California. Cline, who was ninety-six when I talked to him and just retired from his law practice in Wharton, Texas, remembers asking one question he felt turned the case around for him. A military policeman said that Robinson had told him, "If you call me a nigger one more time, I'll break your back." Clines said he found that interesting. He asked the military policeman:

"Did you refer to Robinson as a nigger?"

"No, sir, I never did that."

"Why did Robinson tell you what he would do if you referred to him as a nigger?"

"I don't rightly know, sir," the man answered.

The court-martial board did not buy that. Of course the guard called him that name. The case fell apart. The jury was out for about a half hour and Robinson was found not guilty on all charges.

CHAPTER THREE

Branch Rickey never changes his tale. The fire in him to fix a nation began in 1904 on the practice fields at Ohio Wesleyan University, where he first saw Charlie Thomas play baseball.

There is an away game against the University of Notre Dame at South Bend, Indiana. Rickey, as student coach, booked his team into the Oliver Hotel there. Reservations were made well in advance. The hotel was delighted. After all, these were fine Methodists coming in. Maybe they weren't Catholics, but they knew how to behave.

The catcher for Rickey's team is Charlie Thomas. His sloping shoulders and thick neck proclaim him a hitter. The big, young black hands are those of a catcher. Charlie Thomas is the first of his race ever to play at Ohio Wesleyan. This puts the school only a half-century ahead of the good Catholics of Notre Dame.

The Ohio Wesleyan players came into the hotel cheerfully, Charlie Thomas among them. Then they reached the room clerk, whom Rickey described as being ready to defend his hotel to the death rather than let this young black man inside. The clerk suggested that Thomas go to the YMCA. Instead, Rickey sent the team manager to the Y to see about lodging for the entire squad. He reported back quickly that there were no rooms. Thomas, humiliated, said he would go back to school. Rickey took his arm and told him he was staying. He asked to see the hotel manager and mesmerized the fellow, reaching an agreement that Thomas could stay in Rickey's room until a suitable black family was found to house him. No such thing was ever going to happen. Rickey took Thomas up to his room, then ordered a cot and called down to the manager, "Under no circumstances will I allow Thomas to leave."

Thomas sat in Rickey's room and began crying. He rubbed one big hand over the other, saying, "Black skin, black skin. If I only could rub it off and make it white."

Rickey said, "Stop it. If you can't beat this, how do you expect me to?"

Rickey is out of the mud and stone of Scioto County in Ohio's southland. On his mother's side, the Brown family was among the first Americans, one of eight families that sailed from Scotland to Massachusetts in 1646. The head of the Brown family, Daniel, had a grandson, George, who founded the Methodist Church in America. Rickey's great-grandfather, David Brown, seemed off to a smashing start, too. He married Sallie Hubbard, whose family were weathly landowners that included a member of President Millard Fillmore's cabinet. But David did not quite fit in. He drank anything in a bottle and fought anybody who happened to be nearby, whether in a church pew or in somebody's parlor. He mortified his wife every sundown, when his thirst arose. He slipped through her passionate lectures against the drink and came out the other side clutching a bottle, his free hand in a fist. Any mention of politics was the sure start of a brawl. He said he was a Democrat and showed his loyalty to Andrew Jackson by breaking a leg in an election-day scuffle.

David went west with a pregnant wife and a quarter to his name. They went by horse and wagon to Pittsburgh, and then aboard a raft on the Ohio River to Sciotoville. The population was somewhat over zero. They had four children before going farther into the wilderness with a baby strapped to the side of the ox wagon. His wife, Sallie, had the reins. David walked ahead, chopping brush and trees with an ax. They stayed there for a decade, raising vegetables. Sallie had great faith in Jesus as the savior of all, and spread this wherever she went.

Their granddaughter Emily married a farmer's son, Jacob Franklin Rickey. The Rickeys came out of Tioga, New York, Baptists turned Wesleyan Methodists. Frank and Emily settled in Madison Township, Ohio, and had a family, including a son, Wesley Branch Rickey, born in December 1881.

Branch and his older brother, Orla, attended a school that was a four-mile walk from home. There was a bookstore fire in nearby Portsmouth, and the father bought eleven damaged books for a hard-to-come-by $2.25. He purchased Dante's *Inferno*, and *The Story of the Bible* and the New Testament and four volumes of Washington Irving. The father worked on his sons' reading and the mother on their belief in God.

On sandlot fields of Ohio, young farm people played

for their towns, Turkey Creek and Duck Run and Lucas-ville. They paid a dollar for a bat and a nickel for a "Nickel Rocket," which was a baseball that wasn't worth a dime. An official National League baseball went for a hard dollar and a quarter. The face mask Branch wore cost fifty cents and yielded to any foul tip or wild pitch, almost giving him a new face. His next mask cost four dollars and was the first thing that he grabbed at the end of a game so it wouldn't be lost or stolen.

Years later, one of Rickey's granddaughters, going through the oldest of old files and clippings from *The Columbus Dispatch* and *The Cincinnati Enquirer*, noticed accounts of people remembering her grandfather playing in a big game in town. Rickey crouches and catches for Orla, a powerful pitcher for Duck Run, against Dry Run. With the bases loaded in the final inning, Branch called for Orla's big one. The pitch was big and fast and high, too high for Branch to catch. It sailed over his head, and while he ran to get it three runs raced across the plate. Branch picked up the ball, saw the game was over, and walked straight home. It was a defeat that sat down in his mind and never got up.

Fifty years on, it is a glorious afternoon at Yankee Stadium in New York, shimmering with World Series tension, and simultaneously roars come up from the stadium's three packed tiers. Pigeons carrying film circle and then fly into the sky to the newspaper plants downtown. Rickey runs the St. Louis Cardinals, and he has one of the left-handers he loved, Ernie White, up from his famous farm teams, shutting out the Yankees. Shutting out the Yankees in the World Series. Shut them out for nine innings, because in those years pitchers worked a full game. White's pitches went over nobody's head. He cut the Yankees off with curves at the knees. It caused Rickey to reminisce in the newspapers about brother Orla's pitch.

That Cardinal team of 1942 was Rickey's, from the first day in spring to the last of fall. It was Rickey's team right to the uniform shirtfront featuring a pair of redbirds perched on a black baseball bat, copied from a sketch on a napkin left at a women's luncheon. It might have been the best team baseball ever had, down to the rookie he decided to put in the outfield, a kid named Stanley Frank Musial.

Next the Rickey family moved from Duck Run to Lucasville, population 150, because it had schoolrooms in a building, not a shack. The father continued his obsession with his sons' reading. Rickey's regular education in Duck Run had required long hours reading at the kitchen table. Many other families did not, or could not, read or write. When Branch came to Lucasville classrooms he was so shy that others believed him to be bone stupid. He immediately began to stutter. It took months of painstaking tutoring by James Finney, an Ohio Wesleyan teacher in training, to cure it. He slowed Rickey's breathing and tongue. He also left an Ohio Wesleyan logo imprinted on Rickey's mind.

Outside the classroom, Rickey learned a different lesson. This came in the form of the electric shock he received when Jane Moulton, daughter of the owner of Lucasville's general store, left a Valentine card under his door. Until then, Jane had been the fastest runner of all the girls in school. Her interest in finish lines waned as she began walking with Rickey. The Moulton family store had a sign stating, "Frugality, industry and sobriety are simple virtues any man can cultivate." Rickey's family motto was "Make things first, seek the Kingdom of God and make yourself an example."

If it had been left to Rickey's upbringing, he never would have seen Charlie Thomas or even a college classroom. Rickey goes to college against his father's will. Right up to the son's last dawn at home, his father insisted that he should be helping on the farm.

Jane Moulton attended college in Oxford, Ohio, and that was enough for Rickey. He applied to Ohio Wesleyan in the nearby town of Delaware. His baseball catching and football skills were not harmful to his application. At 5:00 a.m. of a chill March morning in 1901, he had breakfast, then took a newspaper, rolled it up, tied a string around it, kissed his mother good-bye, and was off to the railroad tracks. He stood alongside the rails until he heard a train coming out of the darkness. He lit the newspaper and swung it as a torch. The Norfolk and Western train headed for the state capital, Columbus, stopped for him, and he was on his way.

Ohio Wesleyan had twelve hundred students, mostly from deeply religious Midwestern families. Tuition they charged him was five dollars per semester. For another 50 cents a week, Rickey got a room so small his toes rested against a wall when he slept. In his first day of Latin class, the professor, John Grove, asked Rickey to read from Virgil. Rickey got up, missed words, and stuttered. Grove asked which grammar book he had studied before and Rickey blurted, "Yours." Which was true. But Branch hadn't attended high school and knew Grove's book only from study at the kitchen table. The class shrieked with laughter, which stung Rickey to tears. In his mind he ran over the timetable of trains home; he had arrived with the Norfolk and Western schedule memorized. The next one to Lucasville was 2:10 and he was going to be on it.

The professor, however, was one of those who thought he was supposed to teach. He told Rickey to show up at 7:30 each morning for special help. This turned Rickey into a grateful Latin student. He now practiced his kitchen-table study habits on library wood and beneath real lighting, with great results. To survive, he waited on tables, which put him close to food, and tended furnaces.

One winter night I am in Delaware, Ohio, at the college library, and the librarian brings out envelopes holding the details of Rickey's life at the school. In one of them is a letter that Rickey wrote to an Ohio Wesleyan administrator in 1952.

"I never did go to high school and never saw the inside of one until after I went to Delaware," Rickey wrote. "I was a preparatory student with two years of so-called prep work to do in order to become a freshman. I carried as many as twenty-one hours in one term and never did catch up with any class until the spring term of 1904. As you know, I did the preparatory work and the four years of college work in 3⅓ years. I often felt that I did not deserve my Bachelor of Literature degree because in many respects I did not work hard enough . . . No boy could have had less money than I had in my first year in college . . . During my first term at Delaware I had one pair of pants, and only one pair of pants, and nobody saw me wear anything else. I cleaned them myself and pressed them myself, and not infrequently, and they saw me through."

The YMCA in Delaware, Ohio, had a speakers' program set up by its part-time secretary, Branch Rickey. They brought in figures such as Jane Addams, Jacob Riis, and Booker T. Washington, who delivered a detailed report on the condition of blacks in America. He was the first man of color Rickey ever heard speaking so. Usually, the role of judging black character was white work.

Rickey spent the summer of 1903 with the Terre Haute team of the Central League and then stepped up to LeMars of the Iowa–South Dakota League. He was now climbing organized baseball's shaky ladder. The Dallas team of the Texas League was without a catcher and somehow Rickey contacted them. They sent a telegram telling him to show up within three days. He could get $175 a month, which back then was bank robbery money. He took bus and train, but would have run if necessary. At Dallas he caught 41 games and hit .261.

By late August he was brought up to the big-league club, the Cincinnati Reds. He was twenty-two. Rickey walked on the field in awe and whistled in the clubhouse.

His mother had made one restriction. Professional baseball was the Devil's playground, the woman believed. She saw Satan prancing in the infield. She made Branch promise that he would never be in a baseball park on a Sunday. He made that the vow of a lifetime. "People believed it was a deep religious matter, but it wasn't that at all," his grandson Branch III says. "It was a promise to his mother. He kept it."

On a searing August Sunday, the Cincinnati Reds dressed and took the field without their rookie catcher. Manager Joe Kelley made inquiries. "He takes Sunday off," somebody said.

"Tell him don't come back," Kelley said.

Rickey went to the club owner, Garry Herrmann, a Republican-machine politician with an office in City Hall. Herrmann was sympathetic from the handshake. The reason why people are in the best hands when they give their problems to a politician is that the man does favors for a living. He asked Kelley to take Rickey back. When Rickey came to the dressing room, Kelley fumed and refused to let him in. Rickey went back to Herrmann. The politician could never let Rickey go away thinking that he had failed to deliver. He gave Branch $306.50 for his prorated monthly salary. It was the most money Rickey had ever earned, and he went home excitedly showing the check.

"If we pay him, we must use him," Herrmann told Kelley, who sighed and allowed Rickey back in the clubhouse.

Rickey remained there until the next Sunday, when he went home to church again. Kelley told the owner, "This guy is making a fool out of us." Rickey was gone by nightfall, his contract sold to Charles Comiskey, who had just bought the Chicago White Sox. Rickey asked to have a guarantee in his contract that he could have Sundays off. When he told Comiskey that this was because of a promise to his mother, Comiskey sobbed and wrote in the Sunday clause. When his manager heard, he told Comiskey, "I know Rickey is a religious fanatic, but I didn't think you were." The agreement soon ended.

Rickey was sent to the St. Louis Browns, where he made his first major league appearance as a hitter. He faced Rube Waddell of the Philadelphia Athletics. Waddell threw three pitches. Rickey wasn't sure he saw them. The umpire was certain. He said they were strikes. By 1906 Rickey had become a catcher for the New York Highlanders of the American League, who would rename themselves the Yankees. He was paid $2,700. The games were played on a bluff overlooking the Hudson River at 165th and Broadway, now the grounds of New York–Presbyterian Hospital. Rickey stayed at the Fifth Avenue Hotel down on 23rd Street. Across the street was the Eden Museum, at whose front entrance was a robot checkers player named Ajeeb. The robot was dressed in what the museum claimed was an East Indian outfit. A customer named Tighe, as quoted in the *World* newspaper, noted, "I never knew India had an East Side." The robot's clawlike hands were directed by a guy at a governing board looking down from one flight up. Rickey had a checkerboard set up permanently in his house and couldn't pass up the chance to beat a robot. He played Ajeeb so many times, and lost so noisily, that a crowd gathered each night to watch. One night Rickey finally had victory in hand. "I've got you now," he shouted at the robot. "Try making a move." Ajeeb blew a fuse.

Rickey got to the ballpark by taking the new subway, which then went only as far as 137th Street, and boarding a horsecar for the rest. He got off that cart the first time with an arm that felt leaden and achy. Twinges turned into full pain when he tried to throw. The team put him in anyway; they didn't have another catcher. Early in Rickey's first game somebody tried to steal on him. Rickey threw into right field. Thirteen runners stole bases on him that day. Soon he didn't even try throwing. That sent him back to his new wife, the former Jane Moulton, who was a long bus ride away in Ohio.

Back home, he lived life in a constant rush. He coached baseball at Ohio Wesleyan and took law-school classes at night at Ohio State University, forty miles and more away. When his favorite teacher at Ohio Wesleyan became ill, he took over the man's class in elementary law and refused to accept any money, assuring that the teacher's family could continue to receive his salary.

For an immensely powerful man, he was vulnerable to tuberculosis and Ménière's disease of the inner ear. He ignored the first serious symptoms of illness while throwing himself into the 1908 presidential campaign of William Howard Taft, also from Ohio. Signs of exhaustion began coming earlier each day. Still, he drove through nights to stand on boxes in town squares in Portsmouth and Chillicothe and Akron, and to praise Taft to the heavens. He made sure to include a snide attack on the drink. His sponsor for this part of the show came from some Ohio Anti-Saloon League. Soon the coughing had him spitting blood. The first country doctor he saw said it was tuberculosis. At this time in America, in a survey taken in 1905, some 10 percent of deaths were caused by TB.

The illness left Rickey on the ground, bundled in blankets, breathing the freezing night air in a sanitarium at

Saranac Lake, a mountain slum in the Adirondacks in upstate New York. The hospital was founded by a doctor, Edward Livingston Trudeau, who had lived with a brother who came down with tuberculosis. They shut themselves in a dark airless room because the wisdom of the time was that fresh air would make you cough yourself to death. Of course the airless room killed Trudeau's brother and soon sent the doctor, sick and wheezing, to the mountains so he would have some scenery while dying. When the mountain air saved him, he was so thankful that he established his sanitarium there. Rickey became a patient and he, too, survived.

While he was recovering, he received an admissions letter from the University of Michigan Law School. He left Saranac with a song in his throat. "It was a complete cure," Rickey announced upon his return to Michigan.

Photographs show that when Rickey got to Ann Arbor after his tuberculosis treatment at Saranac, he reached for a big cigar to celebrate. He smoked these cigars for the next half century. Sometimes they stayed unlit and were comfortable props. But sometimes they were steaming; a photo on a book jacket shows his face covered with smoke.

At that time, famous people were paid to show you how to smoke stylishly, and kept cancer a myth. The newspapers and radio shows and the sports teams all were tied in with the tobacco companies. Drive somewhere and the billboards featured movie stars who looked good smoking. It was called a miracle in engineering when out of a huge Camel cigarette billboard in Times Square there came perfect smoke rings maybe three stories high blown from the mouth of a delighted smoker. Thousands each day stood in the street to watch the smoke rings come into the air. They learned to hate the wind.

People died frightful deaths of cancer, but newspaper obits told only of "a lengthy illness." Cancer was the secret word all the way to 1946 when Damon Runyon died of throat cancer at the Sloan-Kettering Institute in Manhattan. A fight manager, Eddie Walker, took a call in the hallway from Joseph Hertzberg, city editor of the *New York Herald Tribune* newspaper. "What was the cause of death?" Hertzberg asked.

"Cancer," Eddie Walker said.

The word appeared in the paper in the morning and became the first time that anybody famous was listed as dying of the disease. Runyon, who put so many phrases into the American language, now took one out. "Lengthy illness" was gone.

Rickey's influence on others might have been wasted, you can argue, by his overrating the damage done by alcohol. If you made a list of all the earthly evils, drink might wind up near the bottom. Smoke, greed, and envy are at the top. Rickey never understood the relaxation that accompanied a cold beer at a bar. Or a big drink of whiskey at the end of another day that had allowed no pleasure. Alcohol at its worst hurts people. Cancer still kills.

Instead, Rickey's sport was sponsored by P. Lorillard, makers of Old Gold cigarettes. A home run was called "An Old Goldie." As the runner went around the bases after hitting one, a carton of Old Golds tumbled down the netting behind home plate. A batboy ran up, snatched the carton of smokes, and ran it to the players' dugout. As a prize, the home run hitter was given a shot at lung cancer.

I am in the city room of the old *New York Herald Tribune* and writing to my rhythm: go to the coffee container on the left and then to the black Underwood typewriter in the middle. The words are painful and as I read them a robot hand goes to the right, to a smoking Pall Mall on the edge of the desk. You take the cigarette, then study the last words through the exhaled smoke. You put it together—coffee, two-finger typing, Pall Mall—you have my assembly line.

This woman is in the front of the room staring at me. She is just coming from seeing the editors on some matter. Suddenly she walks past desks and comes up to me.

"Hello, I'm Mary McLaughlin. I'm the health commissioner."

"That's nice."

"I just want to say one thing. How many cigarettes are you smoking?"

"Two packs." I lie. I smoke three packs of Pall Malls every day. Two for work. And then I need a full pack on the bar in front of me after work.

"Would you mind if I told you one thing? You would be better off on a one-hundred-fifty-dollar-a-day heroin habit than you are now."

She was a civilized woman. She made her point and did not show off. She left me retching over cigarettes that I could not quit until I caught a flu and missed work for the only time in my life, for three days, and then I bought cigarettes on Myrtle Avenue and I took the first drag and my chest heaved and I threw up. I have not had a cigarette since that moment. Oh, it was a miracle. 1968.

Rickey finished law school near the top of his class. The university's athletic department offered him a job, which he turned down because he was about to open a law practice in Boise, Idaho, with two fraternity brothers from Ohio Wesleyan. He wanted Boise because he was sure the cold air would benefit his health. And he even had a client. He was assigned to defend somebody who, as Rickey recalled, "was charged with more crimes than I thought could be committed by one person." Years later, Rickey was having lunch at the Union League Club in Manhattan when an old man came to his table and said, "I'm Judge Davis of Boise, Idaho. Just wanted to shake your hand. I heard your first case and you lost it." The judge thought this was great sport, having something over on a big guy. His appearance was evidence of why they should have extensive psychiatric testing for people to whom you allow power. The client in Boise also seems to be the only one in memory. Rickey did not even have a nice old widow to advise.

He soon wired the Michigan athletic department: "Am starving. Will be back without delay."

He returned to Michigan as baseball coach, arriving just in time to interview incoming student-athletes, including one who changed his life. Rickey recounted his first meeting with this young man to his assistant, Arthur Mann:

Candidates for several varsity baseball teams were reporting for registration, assignment and tryout.

Here before me stood a handsome boy of 18 with dark brown hair, serious gray eyes, and good posture. He was about five feet eight or nine, well built but not heavy, and he wore a somewhat battered finger glove on his right hand. He said he pitched on a high school team in Akron, Ohio, and that he was George Sisler, engineering student in the freshman class.

"Oh, a freshman," I said. "Well, this part of the program is only for the varsity." He showed extreme disappointment. I said, "You can't play this year, but you can work out with the varsity today."

The undergraduate news gathering of *The Michigan Daily* was at its best in the spring of 1912 when its stringer covering intramural sports was present at a game in which the freshman engineering students played the school's varsity. The game became famous because of the pitcher for the freshman engineers. The newspaper proclaimed his pitching success under this old-time headline style:

UNEARTH 'FIND' IN INTERCLASS GAME
Sisler, Freshman Engineer, Twirls for
Seven Innings and Strikes Out Twenty Men

The next time Sisler pitched, students came running from all over campus to watch. When they got to the baseball field, they found Rickey, who plainly did not want to be bothered while he was doing the important work of measuring Sisler's ability. The more Rickey watched him pitch, the deeper grew his belief that this boy was for the ages.

Added to this, Sisler could hit. Rickey admitted later that he almost fainted with excitement. Sisler was still a freshman and ineligible to play on the varsity until his second year. So he was out of Rickey's hands when he went home for the summer and met with a scout, which was worse than finding a serious girl.

"Did you ever sign anything?" Rickey asked him.

"No," said Sisler. "Just some letter saying I'd pitch for this Akron team."

"Did he pay you?"

"No, I said I didn't want money right now. So I didn't really sign anything."

"Yes, you did," Rickey said. "A baseball contract."

Rickey opened his law books and proclaimed that all of America's youth would be endangered if such cradle robbing were allowed. "You must not force recognition of this illegal contract," Rickey told the commissioner of baseball at the time. "If you do this you will forever alienate parents and colleges and even high schools."

Before long, Rickey was hired as manager of the St. Louis Browns baseball team. Of course he brought George Sisler along with him. Henrietta Slote of the University of Michigan Law School states today that it is the school's belief that Branch Rickey's theft of Sisler "dwarfs the Jackie Robinson business."

CHAPTER FOUR

Branch Rickey invented the baseball farm system, which gathered players of promise and grew them, like crops, on minor league teams, or farm clubs. The practice was modeled somewhat after the Southern system of slavery, but that was all right because it was baseball and the sport had its own quaint beliefs. It was in Alabama in 1913 that Rickey and the St. Louis Browns owner, Colonel Bob Hedges, got four Montgomery businessmen together and bought the local baseball team. The agreement was that Rickey and Hedges would stock the team with prospects. At season's end, they could buy the contracts of as many players as they liked, each for $1,000. This was a small amount of money to pay for seasoned players—too small, one of the team owners said. As this man was operating in the state capital, he leaned heavily to larceny. When Rickey and Hedges discovered they were objects of an attempted robbery, they dropped the arrangement.

St. Louis at this time had the most inept baseball players gathered in one place since the invention of foul lines. The Browns lost 99 games in one season. Their crosstown rivals, the Cardinals, were worse. Out of carnage like this arises great opportunity. The owner of the Cardinals,

Mrs. Helene Britton, stood in her bedroom one night and considered her life. She didn't want to face the next morning because all her team did was lose. She looked around at her husband, Schuyler Britton. He was in pajamas. She despised him. She despised him worse than she did losing baseball games.

The following day, Mrs. Britton sent a team of divorce lawyers into court to start proceedings. Later, a second group of lawyers and financial people were told to find a buyer for the Cardinals. She never wanted to see the team or her husband again. It was a parlay that made her life easier.

Soon the Browns were sold to one Phil Ball, who replaced Rickey as manager not long after Rickey returned from overseas. His baseball career had been interrupted in 1918 by World War I, during which he served as an officer in the 1st Gas Regiment, a chemical-assault unit. Ball's decision opened the way for Rickey to go across the street to the Cardinals. He ran that franchise for the next seventeen years.

From the start he went right back to his notion of a farm system. On behalf of the Cardinals, he bought teams all over the country. Year in and out he signed players until he had 650 minor league prospects stocking teams of varying heft from Houston, Texas, to Syracuse, New York, to Topeka, Kansas, and points in between. Creating an army of prospects from which he could replenish the roster of the big-league team, Branch Rickey changed the look of baseball long before he ever heard of Jackie Robinson, so much so that Kenesaw Mountain Landis, baseball's commissioner, became Rickey's mortal enemy.

In one ruling, Landis said no player signed by a major league team could be sent to the minors until he had been given a thorough tryout right at the end of spring training. Rickey howled. The rule stayed. There were more such rules inspired by Rickey's farm system, which was generally known as "The Chain Gang." Players were bought and sold and assigned to teams without being asked. Not everyone was unhappy about it. The opinion of many sports people was, "These players are being taken out of the gas station and being paid to play. Who are they to complain about anything?"

Branch Rickey was neither a savior nor a samaritan. He was a baseball man, and nowhere in his religious training did he take a vow of poverty. There came a day in St. Louis that he looked at his famous first baseman, Johnny Mize, who could hit a ball several miles. Mize had led the league in batting and slugging. That he ran quite slowly was a drawback, except the Cardinals had so much speed that the team could accommodate a man with no feet. But then Rickey saw that Mize had developed a new flaw: he had grown an agent.

"John loves playing in St. Louis," the agent said to Rickey. "If he could just get what he deserves."

Though the Cardinals might have needed Mize's bat, Rickey now saw only a player who wanted more money than he was worth. Seeking to jettison Mize, he approached New York Giants owner Horace Stoneham, a restless drunk whom Rickey found sufferable only because whiskey made the man vulnerable.

"Johnny Mize would add glory to the spires of New

York," he assured Stoneham. In truth, the last thing the Giants needed was an infielder who lumbered. Rickey spoke of the glories of Mize until he had sold the player to Stoneham for $50,000, of which 10 percent went to Rickey. This was above Rickey's salary of $50,000.

He got that 10 percent commission on nearly every player he sold, and he sold hundreds of them, for price tags from a few thousand to one hundred thousand dollars. In the records, there are notices of sales for Bob Bowman ($35,000) and Charles Wilson ($59,000) and Nate Andrews ($7,500) and Don Padgett ($35,000), and you could sit there all night totaling these sales figures, with 10 percent off the top for Rickey. He made his biggest sale in 1938, to Chicago chewing-gum maker Phil Wrigley, when he unloaded one of the greatest players he ever managed.

"Answer me this," Rickey asked his wife, Jane, one night when he came home for dinner. "Would you say I am somewhat intelligent? Would you say that as a result of Ohio Wesleyan and Michigan Law School that I am fairly well educated? Then why did I exhaust myself for four hours today with a person named Dizzy?"

Jerome Dean was a big, loose kid who ran out to the mound in the Shawnee, Oklahoma, tryout camp of the St. Louis Cardinals. He was six foot four and it appeared that he might be able to throw fast. This was late in the 1930 season. He would have been there earlier except the Cardinals' scout for his region, Don Curtis, worked only part-time for the baseball team and full-time with the Missouri, Kansas & Texas Railroad, and he was sorry but the rail schedule didn't allow him time to watch the kid pitch for the San Antonio Power and Light Company and bring him around until now.

Rickey, with a floppy canvas hat covering him from the sun, leaned forward to get a better look as Dean took the mound. A line of batters, hoping desperately to get the hits that would bring a contract, waited to face him.

On the mound, Jerome Dean raised his leg and threw. The first pitch was a fastball. He threw eight more to make three outs. Nobody even got a foul tip.

Rickey spoke quietly. Keep this kid out there for the next three batters. They did. Dean threw nine more strikes and still nobody touched the ball. Rickey's face and voice revealed nothing. Inside, he was experiencing the sensation that ran through him when he first saw George Sisler pitch and then swing a bat. If he said out loud what he was thinking now, that we are dealing here with a star who looks like he will still be a name in the next century, somebody would tell this kid and the first thing the kid would do is demand a freight car full of money. And Rickey couldn't have that.

He signed Dean for money suitable for counting on a candy-store counter and sent him to St. Joseph, Missouri, in the Western League. Dean won twenty-six games and was in St. Louis by the end of the season.

"Just tell the boys to get a couple of runs and I'll take care of the rest," he announced. That happened. They let him pitch and in his first major league game he suffered misfortune by allowing three Pirates to get hits. At the hotel late that night he inspected the top paper on a bundle of first editions of the *St. Louis Post-Dispatch*. "Damn!" he called out as he saw his picture big and smiling on the first page.

Rickey leaned on Oliver French, the general manager of the St. Joseph team, to take Dean into his home over the fall and winter. The Frenches found Dean charming but raucous: they had trouble sleeping when he went down in the cellar and threw pieces of coal into the open furnace.

Dean left the house one day and made his way to Rickey's office in St. Louis. He needed $150.

"He didn't give me any money," Dean reported of the conversation that followed. "All I got was a lecture on sex."

Dean once rented a car and drove it until it ran out of gas in the countryside. He left the vehicle there and hitchhiked back home. The rental agency had to send out a scout to find the car and they billed Dean $300. He not only couldn't pay, he wouldn't.

Dean was a four-time All-Star and led Rickey's Cardinals to a World Series win in 1934. A few years after that, Rickey sold him to Wrigley for $185,000, of which Rickey took his usual 10 percent.

By the time Rickey unloaded Dean, the pitcher's arm was largely shot, but four years later he made a move that wasn't nearly as shrewd. Rickey didn't need to travel far to find Yogi Berra and bring him to a workout at Sportsman Park. The catcher was a short, stocky, earnest guy who came out of the Hill District in St. Louis and could reach over his head and swat a pitch into next week. Casey Stengel said of him, "He acts like he's not very smart. But he's got a very good sports mind, which is good for a player to have."

Yogi became Rickey's biggest mistake. Berra remembered this one day at an affair in his hometown, Montclair,

New Jersey: "Jack Maguire, who was scouting for St. Louis, took me to a tryout Rickey ran with the Cardinals. He offered Joe Garagiola five hundred and then he watched me and said he would give me two hundred fifty. I wouldn't sign with him. He was going to the Dodgers the next year. He told the Cardinals that I wasn't so good. He wanted me with Brooklyn. At the end of the year he sent me a telegram saying I had to report to the Dodgers camp at Bear Mountain. I never did. I wasn't signed. I guess he still didn't believe I wouldn't sign with him. He figured he had talked me out of every place but his. So many people saw me playing that the Yankees heard I was good. That's where I went."

We are now at the end of the 1942 season. Three years before this Rickey and the Cardinals owner, Sam Breadon, had a disagreement that became a bitter dispute that turned into anger that required an awareness of the perpetual need for lawful behavior. It was over money, don't worry about that. Breadon had cut every salary, including the cleaning woman's. Rickey made a Prussian surprise attack and announced that he would leave when his contract ended. The team had just won the World Series, but Breadon did nothing to make Rickey stay. So he left landlocked St. Louis, whose Southern customs blocked his true ambitions, and moved to Brooklyn, which had both feet in the Atlantic Ocean, whose tides slapped the shore and sent foam into the air, the spray and the waves carrying from all corners of the earth.

CHAPTER FIVE

Branch Rickey loved to plan. He walked around with pockets filled with notes, and he would rush to board the train from New York to Philadelphia for a Dodgers road game and sit going through his notes without a dollar on him. Conductors rode him on credit. Once, his wife went shopping at a department store in Dayton, Ohio, while he attended a business meeting nearby. When he was finished, he told the driver to start for home. They were well gone when he suddenly remembered his wife. They rushed back to find her standing wearily on the sidewalk. He went through life carrying notes to himself on slips of paper, coffee shop menus, napkins. He could see months and even years ahead, devising tactics to fit future situations.

In these early years in Brooklyn, he worked on his six-point plan to integrate baseball. By 1945 he had already handled the first point during his meeting with George V.: secure the backing of the team ownership. The remaining five points were: (2) find the right Negro player and (3) find the right Negro *person*; (4) employ public relations; (5) gain support of the Negro community; and (6) gain acceptance by his teammates.

He started working on these points a full two years

before the player arrived, before he even knew who that player would be. At lunch on one particular day, he walked down the street hoping to make some headway on point four, public relations.

Walter "Red" Barber, the radio announcer for Dodger games, met Rickey in Joe's Restaurant on Fulton Street, a few blocks from the Dodgers office. Barber was out of Mississippi and Florida and had a voice to prove it, soft and Southern yet understandable, and calling to mind magnolia blossoms. The voice captured Brooklyn. Red Barber might have been the most literate, the most thrilling, of announcers, calling plays with unforgettable understatement and humor. "We're in the catbird seat," he told listeners. Rickey loved it, but he also knew that all his planning could be useless without Barber's voice on his side. He could hear Barber from every car radio, barbershop, kitchen window. This became his dearest tactic. Proximity! Rickey would hypnotize everyone with Barber's familiar voice carrying the exploits of the new player through the streets of Brooklyn, into Manhattan, and out through Long Island, his Southern voice reassuring all.

The two men sat across from each other at Joe's Restaurant. Breaking salt rolls into crumbs, Rickey immediately told Barber, "Mrs. Rickey and my family say I'm too old at sixty-four, and my health is not up to it. They say I've gone through enough baseball and [taken enough] from the newspapers. That every hand in baseball will be against me. But I'm going to do it."

"He looked straight into my eyes," remembered Barber, "fixing my attention."

Rickey said, "I'm going to bring a Negro to the Brooklyn Dodgers."

Barber remembered Branch Rickey speaking slowly as he said it: "I'm going to bring a Negro to the Brooklyn Dodgers."

Barber sat straight and silent.

"I don't know who he is," continued Rickey, "or where he is, but he is coming."

From somewhere, small sounds rose through Barber's memory and became loud and formed a crowd in Sanford, Florida. A harsh, bare, hot sun burned down from above. Red Barber, age ten, was on the edge of a crowd of jeering, nasty men in Ku Klux Klan robes. They shoved a black man, crying, tarred and feathered, along the streets. Barber was told that he was witnessing a great event.

In remembering this, Barber always quoted the one line that might be the best written in English in our time: "I had been carefully taught."

Now Barber was witness to a truly great event, Branch Rickey's assault on ignorance. "All the men in baseball understood the code," Barber recalled later. "A code is harder to break than an actual law. A law is impersonal. Often a man breaks a law, is clever enough to get away with it, and people think he is a smart fellow. But when you break an unwritten law, a code of conduct, you are damned, castigated, banished from the club so to speak. You are a renegade, a scoundrel, an ingrate, a pariah."

Leaving Joe's that day, Barber felt that lesson becoming heavier and harder. He walked across to the subway, took it to Grand Central Station, and there in the vast splendor, with so many people walking quickly by him at the end of a day's business, he told himself that he couldn't do it. He wouldn't announce a game with a black in it. He reasoned to himself that he always hung out with players before the game, after it, at dinner. This habit gave him anecdotes for his broadcasts. He never could do this with a black player. Nope. He took the train home to Scarsdale.

He walked into the house calling out to his wife, Lylah, that he was quitting. Had to quit. He thought he should call Rickey right now and end it. Lylah Barber thought about that. She was from as far south as her husband was. She also knew that she had a nice, expensive house in southern Westchester County. She was an adult.

She said, brightly, "You don't have to quit tonight. You can do that tomorrow. . . . Let's have a martini." Lylah mixed her husband a big glass of gin and some ice. When he drank it, and allowed that he might have another, she relaxed and had one herself. Barber wasn't going anywhere.

It was somewhere around this time that Jackie Robinson, with all his strength and intelligence, was going around on tryouts. They were destined to break his heart. He went to Fenway Park in Boston accompanied by the baseball writer Wendell Smith, who was trying to help. There was a clubhouse attendant who let them into the park and a batboy or a groundskeeper operating the pitching machine. You had Jackie Robinson ready to show what he could do and nobody wanted to watch. Robinson hit a few and decided to leave. Somebody called good-bye as they left. The Red Sox owner, Tom Yawkey, would spend the next twenty years keeping blacks off his teams and he got what he deserved, which was nothing. He made it in life thanks to his family's huge lumber business, never having to lift a board himself. This was a background similar to those of other baseball owners. Only a few of them, including Rickey and George McLaughlin, appear to ever have done a day's work. This type of experience seemed to mean something. Dan Topping of the Yankees knew what it was like to be shot at in a war, and Chicago's Bill Veeck, who lost a foot in battle in the Pacific, not only wanted to play a black, but was ready to play an all-black team.

"He has to be playing somewhere," Rickey told every scout who came through his office. "Where can we find him?" He went to everybody he knew in baseball at every level, old ballplayers, ministers with athletic fields behind their churches, teachers, old friends who knew a ballplayer when they saw one. He asked all his people to look for blacks. It was that simple. Out on some sandlot, a scout said, "Mister Rickey needs Negroes. I guess we go over the other side of town. That's where they all play."

Branch Rickey read dispatches that came to him from the hundreds of sandlots and fields in the unknown neighborhoods where blacks played. Soon his desk had a stack of reports. One came under the name Robinson. But there were others, too—Campanella, Newcombe, Doby.

He asked his secretary to call Clyde Sukeforth. Now we are getting into it. Sukeforth was a scout who could go out for coffee and come back with a second baseman. Like Rickey, he was an old major league catcher, with Cincinnati and Brooklyn, which to Rickey meant Clyde could see the whole field. His playing days all but ended when he was out hunting in Ohio and birdshot from a misbehaving shotgun ruined his eyes. Yet in the end he could see through a stack of hay and look at a ballplayer on the field and make the decisive judgment on him. He could go beyond running and hitting and measure the character of the player. On a matter of supreme importance, Sukeforth would have the last look and all would hold their breath until he reported to Rickey. Sukeforth called him "Mister Rickey," and the two never relied on each other as heavily as they did during this time.

Sukeforth was born in Washington, Maine. In his later years, he moved to Waldoboro, which was just over the town line. People in Waldoboro said, "He's from away." He attended Georgetown University in Washington, D.C., a powerful institution the mention of which caused Rickey to grunt in approval. Georgetown! Jesuits! Sukeforth had the capacity to go off the baseball field and negotiate delicate matters.

Rickey said years later, of Robinson, "I think we know about his playing ability. I want to begin to know what he is like as a person. He is out of UCLA, an excellent, excellent institution of higher learning and a commissioned army officer. Sukeforth had the capacity to talk to such a man and report to us."

As soon as Rickey read the report on Robinson, he told Sukeforth to find out about the court-martial. Word came back that it was about Robinson refusing to sit in the back of a bus in Fort Hood, Texas.

"He has spirit!" Rickey said with great enthusiasm when he learned the details. "I want you to see Jackie Robinson play shortstop," he told Sukeforth. "He is with the Kansas City team in the Negro league. They are playing at Comiskey Park on the weekend. I want to know about his arm. He certainly is a prospect."

Rickey, obsessed, made many phone calls about Robinson. Each time, some old guy on the other end of the line told him that, yes, Robinson could play in the major leagues. Rickey told Sukeforth, "George Sisler says he never saw anybody protect the plate with two strikes as well as Robinson can. Andy High thought he is the best bunter he ever saw. I want you to talk to him and see if he can come to Brooklyn with you. If he can't, tell him I would be glad to come out and see him."

Clyde Sukeforth's business trip by train to Chicago was so much more than a search for a baseball player. He was not traveling merely to see a baseball player, even a great player, for even these are merely bodies that one day run fast and then run slow before fading into memory. Sukeforth took the train to Chicago and arrived at Comiskey Park on the night of August 24, 1945. He bought a box seat and a program for the Negro League game between the Lincoln Giants and the Kansas City Monarchs. The Kansas City team was coming out of the dugout, and Sukeforth tried to pick Robinson out by his uniform number but decided that the program was usually wrong because the players kept changing. He heard somebody say Robinson's name, and Sukeforth leaned over the rail of the box seat and called to the player.

Sukeforth said right away that he represented Branch Rickey, who was starting a black team. Robinson had soured on Kansas City and listened attentively, although not with great expectations. Then Sukeforth asked Robinson to show him his throwing arm. Robinson hesitated. He had tumbled onto his shoulder a few days before and the arm was still tender. Besides, why did Rickey really want to know about it?

Sukeforth said that Rickey wanted Robinson to come to Brooklyn, but if he couldn't, then Rickey would be pleased to come out to see him.

And with that, everything was different. Standing in the lights of a major league field, rented for the night by blacks, wearing the uniform of a team only blacks knew, Robinson felt a bolt of excitement. Whatever this was about, this fellow Sukeforth made it pleasant. Here was a white man who didn't seem to notice skin color. Robinson observed that Sukeforth spoke quietly when he said that Rickey would travel to see him. He could feel he was being told the truth.

Robinson said he would meet Sukeforth at his hotel, the Stevens, after the game. Sukeforth got to the hotel first and told the desk he was having a guest and then he tipped the elevator operator $2 so he wouldn't balk when a black man rode up. This was only one of the reasons Rickey trusted Sukeforth to handle this job.

Immediately, Sukeforth always said, he knew what he had on his hands. He had read a pound of paper on Robinson. It told of a man born in Cairo, Georgia, which at that time, the late 1910s, was just about the bottom of the country. His mother, Mallie, cleaned houses for white women. When her fifth child, Jackie, was born, she pushed her sharecropper husband to earn more than his $12 a month pay. He sure did. He also ran away.

The mother took her five children on a Jim Crow train to Pasadena, California. Nine days and nights with a baby in your lap and four others writhing about you. She was able to fit her family into a house on Pepper Street, where they were the only black family. The Northern big-city racism came down on them in rocks and screams.

Jackie Robinson came up moody and combative on the streets of Pasadena. The cops actively disliked him. He had a mouth.

An older brother, Mack Robinson, Jackie's hero, had a heart murmur, but he begged to be allowed to run in the 1936 Olympics. He finished second to Jesse Owens and came back from Berlin bitter about not winning. It did nothing to improve Jackie's disposition. Only a person of Branch Rickey's overwhelming personality could calm him.

When he got to schools his athletic ability made him golden. One day he won a broad jump in a meet and then he hitched a ride to the baseball field where he got two hits to win the game. In 1939 and 1940 he was at UCLA, running as a crack halfback who was on All-America lists, performing in front of crowds and being surrounded by admirers and reporters. Sukeforth knew that Robinson had played basketball and run track and was a name in both sports. His legend was already all over the papers on Clyde Sukeforth's lap.

Sukeforth's written report to the Dodgers office noted:

"I asked him why he was discharged from the army and a number of other questions for information we may need. It seemed an old football ankle injury had brought about his discharge but, as it proved, it did not bother him. I reasoned that, if he wasn't going to play for a week, this would be an ideal time to bring up coming to Brooklyn. I had him make a few stretches into the hole in his right and come up throwing. His moves looked good."

Sukeforth had to see a player named Bobby Rhawn in Toledo on Sunday; no matter how important the first player is, you can't make an expensive trip just for one. He asked Robinson if they could meet there and ride the train together to New York. Robinson said yes. Because of his arm, he was taking a few days off from the Monarchs. Suddenly it was real. A magnet was drawing Robinson through the doors and toward a field of mowed grass whose sweetness could be smelled even here. On Sunday, Robinson was at the Toledo ballpark with a bag. Sukeforth bought two spaces in the same Pullman car. The ticket clerk saw a black with him and seemed ready to ask about it. Sukeforth spoke first in words that slapped—yes, they were traveling together.

One of the porters was an organizer for A. Philip Randolph's union of Sleeping Car Porters, which was threatening a major national demonstration over black jobs. He knew Robinson was a college football star. Would he come back in the morning to discuss the march? Robinson agreed, leaving Sukeforth to eat breakfast with the whites, and exciting the workers by telling them he was interested in big-league baseball.

In New York on Monday, Sukeforth went to the Bossert Hotel in Brooklyn and Robinson to the Hotel Theresa, the famous building on the corner of 125th and Seventh Avenue, the cornerstone of Harlem.

They met again at 10:00 a.m. on Tuesday, August 28, 1945, in front of 215 Montague Street in Brooklyn. It is a downtown business street that becomes a place of history. On Montague Street the clothes were seersucker and short sleeves, and bare arms in the August heat. This morning was to become one of the most vividly recalled of these years. All remembering starts with Clyde Sukeforth.

The Brooklyn Dodgers offices were on the corner of Court Street, wide and busy with cars, with the state and federal courts on the far side across from ten- and twelve-story buildings that hold every title guaranty, lawyer, mortgage broker, and insurance broker in the borough. Montague Street starts at Court Street and runs up a street of business offices in low buildings with restaurants on the ground floor. The street goes into a few blocks of the graceful two- and three-story brownstones of Brooklyn Heights. At the end, there is a walk looking over a harbor of glittering water, in the center of which is the Statue of Liberty, which still, today, no matter how many times you have looked at it, takes your breath away.

Sukeforth and Robinson went up to the fourth-floor offices of the Dodgers. The scout was there as third-base coach to history.

They entered Rickey's large office, which had a fish tank and a blackboard with the names in chalk of every member of the Dodgers organization, down to infielders in Olean, New York, Class D.

Rickey sat behind a large desk. Sukeforth said, "Mister Rickey, this is Jack Roosevelt Robinson of the Kansas City Monarchs. I think he is the Brooklyn kind of player."

Rickey put down his cigar and stood up and shook hands. He then sat, and Robinson sat facing him. Off to the side was Sukeforth.

Rickey stared at Robinson.

And stared.

Robinson stared back.

Their eyes cast across a moat of deep silence.

The lawyer in Rickey took over.

"Do you have a contract?"

"No, players only work game by game in the Negro League."

"Do you have anything written or in conversation that ties you to Kansas City?"

"None."

"Do you have a girl?" Rickey asked.

"I think so."

"What do you mean, 'I think so'?"

"Baseball keeps me away so much that I don't know if she's still waiting for me."

"Do you love her?"

"I love her very much."

"Marry her."

He told Robinson that baseball was a hard life and a player had best have a strong home life. Rickey now had the cigar waving, the eyebrows coming together, the eyes piercing even more than before.

"Do you know why we brought you here?"

Robinson said he understood it was for some new Negro baseball team or league.

"No," Rickey told him. "That is not why we went to Chicago for you. You were brought here, Jack Robinson, to play for the Brooklyn organization. We see you starting in Montreal."

Robinson became numb. "Montreal?"

"If you can make it, which everybody says you can. If you make good there, then we'll try you with the Brooklyn Dodgers."

There was more silence. Good, Sukeforth remembered thinking. This puts it where it should be. Everybody knows Robinson's color. We want them talking only about his ability. Sukeforth could think and figure in the silence. Robinson was in clean shock.

Rickey was waving his cigar. With a wave of a cigar he could cure the wound of a lifetime. He was sure of Robinson's baseball ability. He had a pile of reports on Robinson by the most famous scouts, men who could look through a sandlot's dust and see a World Series player. Now Rickey had to learn about the rest. Robinson could control a bat and hit behind a runner. But could he control himself under insults and even assaults and put the attackers to shame? That Sukeforth brought him here said much about his character. But Rickey needed to know even more. It would be easier not to attempt this, he thought.

Robinson couldn't open his mouth. Suddenly, Rickey thumped the desk. "I want to win. I want ballplayers who can win for us. Are you one of them? Do you think you can win for us?"

Robinson had been suspicious of this whole thing. Who was Rickey and what was his record with blacks? But that was before. Now he knew he had to talk; he could not ignore Rickey and what he was saying.

Rickey pounded the desk again.

"Can you?"

"Yes."

"I don't know if you have the guts."

"I'm not afraid of anybody," Robinson said.

"I'm looking for a ballplayer with the guts not to fight back." Off came Rickey's jacket. Now he was the evangelist, the minister roaring and whispering to upturned faces. I know this boy has a soul, Rickey said to himself in this surge of emotion. I am going to bring it forth.

Now Rickey becomes a room clerk. "'We got no room for you, boy. Not even in the coal bin downstairs where you belong.' How would you handle that, Jack Robinson?"

"I guess I go elsewhere."

Now Rickey is a headwaiter who knows that Robinson has just come off a long trip with the team. He doesn't even look at him. Finally, he says. "'Whatchu want, boy?'"

"A seat."

"'Didn't you see a sign at the door says no animals allowed in here?' He turns his back on you. What do you do now, Jack Robinson?"

"Go someplace else to eat, I guess."

Rickey said, "They'll throw at your head."

"They've been throwing at my head for a long time."

Rickey growled. "I'm a player who runs right into you and gets knocked down. I'm getting up and I only see your black face. You knocked me down, you dirty black sonofabitch." Rickey stepped up and threw a fist, a broken baseball catcher's right hand. It just missed grazing Robinson's cheek.

"What do you do now?"

"Mister Rickey, do you want a ballplayer who is afraid to fight back?"

"I said I want a ballplayer with guts enough *not* to fight back. You've got to win this thing with hitting and throwing and fielding ground balls. Nothing else!"

Sukeforth remembered Rickey shivering with tension as he shouted, "We're in the World Series. I'm at first. It's a key part of the game. You are going to throw to first for a double play. And I come into you. You don't give ground. Here are my spikes. You still don't move. You jab that ball into me. I hear the umpire shout, 'Out!' And I see your black face. You dirty black son of a bitch!"

The right hand came at Robinson's face again. He did not move. "His eyes had a lot of sparks in them, I can tell you that," Sukeforth recalled later.

"What do you do?" Rickey asked again.

"Mister Rickey, I've got two cheeks."

It was after lunch, and the afternoon crowd of businessmen was walking by 215 Montague without hearing a murmur of the thunderous American history unfolding nearby. Upstairs, a black man was being signed to a Brooklyn baseball contract that assigned him to the Montreal team of the International League. He would get a signing bonus of $3,500 and a salary of $600 a month. Done.

"First meeting," Branch Rickey began one afternoon when asked what he remembered about this, "lasted about four hours. When he came to me, he came secretly. He came with the idea that he was going to join the Brooklyn Brown Dodgers, a colored entry in the so-called professional colored league . . . And he didn't understand and it was hard for him to believe that day that I had meant for him to become ultimately a member of the Brooklyn club, the Dodgers."

Rickey's plan was to ease Robinson into the league through the Dodgers' farm team in Montreal, "which was a very handsomely acceptable place for the trial of a Negro," he said later. "There is no prejudice in that country. And I knew that. And Brooklyn owned Montreal, and we placed him there on this optional agreement basis.

"Now we had a manager who came from the South, Greenwood, Mississippi. Clay Hopper. Charming fella. Graduated Mississippi A&M. Really, a scholarly type. And fine . . . he was a cotton buyer or sorter working with a dozen other white men and a great number of Negro employees in Greenwood, Mississippi. He was a manager. He was a major league manager in my book . . . If I had a major league club, I wouldn't hesitate to employ him. But this fella felt that his job and his standing and his self-respect was at stake. And I remember that day . . . this fella Robinson made a couple of great plays and I remarked about them and I turned to Hopper on the second one which was a test play, a slide on his belly to the left toward first playing second base he was. He stabbed the ball, kaleidoscopically changed it to the right, retired a front runner at second, and completed a double play from the shortstop to the pitcher. A tremendous play. A test play. A man can do it, you know that he can always do that. And I turned to him . . . and I said there's no man in baseball can beat it. And he turned to me and said, 'Mr. Rickey—' The tears were almost in his eyes. Serious as he could be. 'Do you really believe that he . . . that a colored man'—he didn't really call him that—'a colored man can be a human being?'

"Well, we had to wait for time to change him. Then did it ever!

"Hopper has the player at Montreal. They win the pennant. They carry him, the manager, off on their shoulders. They carry Robinson off on their shoulders. And on his way back to Greenwood, this man just stops in my office . . . He said, 'I'll take only a minute of your time.' He said this fella can make good on your Brooklyn club if you give him a good chance. But he said if he doesn't, Mr. Rickey, he said, don't send him to Hollywood. Don't send him to St. Paul. Let me have him back. He says he's not only a great player, he's a gentle man."

CHAPTER SIX

In the fall of 1945, with Robinson under a contract that was about to be announced, Rickey decided to get out of social engineering for a few moments and pull some money out of the sky. He rented Ebbets Field for a black-versus-white exhibition game. That Sunday in October came up with a light, cold rain. Pitching for the black team was Don Newcombe, nineteen, of the Newark Eagles. He had been told that major league scouts would be watching. He was enthralled. There was one scout there for sure: Clyde Sukeforth sat in a box behind home plate. When Newcombe threw his fastball, Sukeforth watched with eyes that saw something of the pitcher's future. Someday a big winner, the scout thought. And everybody says he can hit.

Newcombe pitched two innings. His arm grew heavier by the throw and throbbed in the rain, and soon he had to get out. He walked off with tears in his eyes. In the dressing room he cried some more. He was sure he had just blown a career. No white scouts were ever going to see him in Newark. Through his tears Newcombe saw one white man in the room. It was Sukeforth, who came up to him and ignored both his color and his tears.

"I like the fastball," Sukeforth said. He asked Newcombe

to be at the Dodgers office in the morning. Newcombe thought it was for the Brown Dodgers team. When they met, Rickey never told him anything different. Just as a day or so later he left Roy Campanella thinking about a Negro league team. Rickey talked for hours but never mentioned the Dodgers except as something attainable someday, maybe. He wanted to know everything about Campanella because he wanted Campanella to handle his Dodgers pitchers, but he couldn't say that yet. Rickey's plan consisted of causing an explosion by signing Robinson to play with Montreal. Once that blew over, he could sign and announce both Campanella and Newcombe.

In January of 1946, Emil "Buzzie" Bavasi returned from three years of infantry fighting in Italy to a job as business manager in the Dodgers farm system. It was good that he had a steady job waiting, but he wasn't ready just yet. He asked Mr. Rickey if he could have some time off to travel to Sea Island, Georgia, to throw the war out of his life and feel the sand on his feet. Of course Rickey said yes.

"Bask in the surroundings and love your wife," he told Bavasi.

A few days later Rickey called and said, "I need you." Bavasi flew up and walked into the Dodgers office in time for a meeting with Rickey and the organization's six top scouts. These men were known wherever anybody played the game: George Sisler, Mickey McConnell, Wid Matthews, Eddie McCarrick, Clyde Sukeforth, and Tom Greenwade. Bavasi made the eighth at the table. The meeting was about the three black prospects—Robinson, pitcher Don Newcombe, and catcher Roy Campanella. All would be brought up through minor league teams. The first would be historic. The other two would follow shortly.

Scouts Andy High and Wid Matthews pushed as forcefully as they knew how for Newcombe to go first.

"He has a powerful arm," Matthews said. "And besides, he is a good hitter. There isn't a pitcher in either league who can hit like he can."

Andy High was even more vehement—Newcombe first.

If the scouts had their way, the team wouldn't be stopping at three black players. When the Montreal team needed a second baseman, Mickey McConnell insisted that they get Jim "Junior" Gilliam of the Baltimore Elite Giants. Rickey said, "Try to acquire him for four thousand." McConnell tried. The Baltimore owner said the team was broke and needed a new bus. For $5,000 Gilliam was Dodgers property, and to acknowledge receipt of their new transportation, Baltimore threw in a pitcher named Joe Black. Sukeforth dived into the pile of files and saw reports that Black was going to win a lot of big-league games.

There would come a day when Sukeforth told Rickey that he had had the greatest luck imaginable: he got two World Series players for $5,000.

Rickey answered, "Luck is the residue of design."

As part of his master plan, Branch Rickey took the sport of baseball into politics, of which nobody in baseball today knows anything beyond giving city council members free box seats. Early on a Sunday in 1945, Rickey and his wife drove up to Quaker Hill, near Pawling, north of the city, a place where there was as much money showing as grass, to visit an old friend from college.

Pherbia and Pinky Thornburg lived splendidly. Pinky had spent many years in China and always was exhilarating in conversation. His wife's brother was a famous radio commentator, Lowell Thomas, who lived nearby. On the grounds of their golf course was a clubhouse called the Barn, which was a large room of high ceilings and dark wood and a stage where Thomas put on Sunday seminars for residents and visitors. On the walls were pictures of the club's Nine Old Men softball team, whose roster included Quaker Hill farm owner Thomas E. Dewey, governor of New York. There were pictures of Dewey, in farmer's overalls hunched forward to pitch, and with Franklin D. Roosevelt, from nearby Hyde Park. One year before Rickey's visit, the two had squared off in a presidential race, and poor suckers all over the country had taken sides, expected to bring at least hatred to the polls. If the voters ever knew that these enemies were happy to be associated with the same softball team of the rich, they might have realized that it was proper to detest them both.

An actress named Tallulah Bankhead, a loud dimwit from Alabama, once proclaimed Dewey to be the "little man on the wedding cake." That caused great giddiness through a couple of elections. But Dewey, the record happens to show, did more for civil rights than any of the giggling Democrats. Branch Rickey knew this as he walked into the clubhouse that Sunday. Here was Thomas E. Dewey, the governor of the state of New York, talking with neighbors. Already, Rickey had met Dewey around state Republican politics. Correct politics were the social conditions for a handshake. But in the informality of the Barn, with Thornburg as his sponsor, Rickey was determined to get help from Dewey. Not jobs for relatives, nor road-paving contracts, nor state grants for the team. Branch Rickey wanted Thomas Dewey to pass a law that would put the first black man into baseball.

In 1943, somewhere in these Sunday seminars in the cabin on Quaker Hill, Irving Ives, a state assemblyman, got a powerful new idea: all working men are created equal, and that includes circus performers and baseball players and anybody else who has to perform in public, and should not be penalized for any reason, including race. He started writing a law to that effect. He merely had to turn around to ask Dewey for help, and he already had a Democratic cosponsor, Elmer Quinn, a state senator from New York City, from Christopher Street in Greenwich Village, St. Veronica's parish.

There was another strong man in the Barn on this day. He was Charles H. Tuttle, a Republican favorite who had run for governor against Franklin D. Roosevelt in 1930. Rickey loved that, as he had no use for any Democrat, and Roosevelt in particular. His hopes lifted even more as he realized that Tuttle had been raised by a grandfather who was the rector of St. Luke's Episcopal Church. Rickey could live with an Episcopalian. Why not? He was already the ally of a Roman Catholic

Right off, Rickey told him the story of Charlie Thomas. "They can't ignore the Constitution like that," Tuttle said.

"We have to fight it," Rickey said.

"Always stand up straight and free," Tuttle said. "Hold fast to your faith and face the future."

Rickey told Tuttle of the St. Louis Browns, whose players were off to war, forcing them to play Pete Gray, a one-armed outfielder, even when there were plenty of blacks with two arms eager to play. When Gray caught a ball, he had to tuck his glove under his stump so he could make the throw. He hit as best he could, which wasn't much, but he was white.

Then they talked about Prohibition, which Tuttle said had harmed thousands of brewery workers, decent people who had to feed their families. For so long, Rickey had believed that working in alcohol was a sin, but now he finally had to admit that Prohibition had been a disastrous failure.

On Monday, Rickey stuffed religious tracts and clippings of talks he had given into a large envelope and sent it to Tuttle. It was the first of many. And it put Rickey into direct touch with a man he felt sure was going to change baseball.

Rickey's hopes also went on the night train with Ives and Quinn to start two weeks of campaigning for passage of their bill in Albany. Opposition came from everywhere. John A. Davis, a Lincoln University professor, had written a handbook calling for gradual integration of Negroes into war industries. He wrote, "Successful companies start their programs with a neat, efficient, attractive, well-qualified colored girl in the employment office itself." Robert Moses came out loudly against the bill. Why a state parks commissioner would be against a fair-employment bill can be explained quickly: he didn't like blacks.

Suddenly appearing in New York shortly thereafter was Senator Robert Taft of Ohio, who wanted to get the same

Republican nomination for president that Dewey was after. Dewey now came out to pass the law for Rickey and Robinson. He spoke to the City-Wide Citizens' Committee on Harlem and told them, "I am standing here with you and you will not see me leaving."

Rickey took advantage of his own proximity to Mayor Fiorello LaGuardia at a ceremony to speak with him about the extreme importance of the bill in Albany. LaGuardia was enthusiastic. He went into his Municipal Building and came up with a young lawyer named Reuben Lazarus, who informed the state legislature that Moses had overreached in his criticism of the state senate bill. The bill was entitled "an act to amend the executive law, in relation to prevention and elimination of practices of discrimination in employment and otherwise against persons because of race, creed, color, or national origin."

The president of the New York State Senate put the question of whether the body would agree to the final passage of said bill. It was decided in the affirmative, a majority of all the senators elected voting in favor thereof and three-fifths being present.

Among those in the great packed senate chamber in Albany was Assemblyman Fred Preller, Queens County Republican. Once, Preller explained to the *Long Island Press* the value of the monthly report he wrote and sent to constituents, single-spaced and printed on both sides of a long sheet of paper. "There are people in my district who are lonely and wait for the mailman," he said. "They have nothing all day but our message. Anybody tells you to shorten it doesn't know Eastern Queens." But he also understood economy of expression under fire. Asked how he was going to vote on the Ives-Quinn bill, he said, "I got a call from the governor's secretary." That's all he said. Many had received that call. The vote in the assembly was 109–32 for the bill.

Rickey had his law.

CHAPTER SEVEN

The former Rachel Isum, with her new last name, Robinson, and her husband, Jackie, flew out of Burbank, California, on February 28, 1946, to join the Montreal team at Dodgers training camp at Daytona Beach, Florida. In his carefully reported biography *Jackie Robinson*, Arnold Rampersad notes, "they reached New Orleans around seven o'clock in the morning. Strolling through the airport, Rachel now saw Jim Crow signs for the first time in her life." On the ladies' room door there was a notice: "Whites."

Of course she went right in, and if the white women in the place were surprised or shocked, that was their problem. The obstacles on the rest of the trip could not be brushed aside so easily. They were bumped from one flight to Florida because whites were given their seats. The next flight, an hour later, left without them. They took a hotel room and the new bride announced that it was not quite right. To her, the bed was a dirty park bench. They did catch a later plane to Pensacola, and when the plane landed they were told to get off because a storm was coming and they had to make the plane lighter. A group of whites, obviously with lighter bones, replaced them.

"Get in the back," a white bus driver said a few hours

later. They had given up on planes and were starting on the bus from Pensacola. Rachel and Jack were crammed into the back with country people caked in dirt and sweat. There were rows of empty seats awaiting decent whites in the front. Every mile was an enemy as the bus went for hour after hour to the Florida east coast. The empty seats in the front of the bus stared at them in mockery.

They arrived in Daytona Beach thirty-six hours after setting out.

Rickey was furious that they were so late, until realizing that for all his planning he had not thought about Jim Crow travel.

At the end of spring training, when the Montreal team was scheduled to play in Baltimore, Frank Shaughnessy, the president of the International League, called Rickey with a voice of pure panic. If Robinson dares play in Baltimore, the public will riot, he bleated.

"Trouble ahead, trouble ahead," Rickey said.

Shaughnessy, who had known Rickey for more than thirty years, persisted.

"Trouble ahead, trouble ahead," Rickey repeated. "If you look for it hard enough you'll find it."

The crowd in Baltimore was so large before the game that Rickey was stuck in the street. After the game, the fans were in a crush around the Royals dressing room. They held out programs for Robinson to sign.

"Yes. There certainly is a riot," Rickey told Shaughnessy on the phone. "It is an autograph riot."

Robinson's first regular season game as the first black in organized baseball was to be played in Jersey City, just across the river from Manhattan. Compared to the medieval south, Jersey City was a highly civilized community. It is one of two American cities that describe their civic philosophies in two words. Chicago's is: "Where's Mine?" Jersey City's: "Not Guilty."

The Jersey City Giants' season opener in April of 1946 was held at Roosevelt Stadium, capacity 24,500. Jackie Robinson started at second base. The day might have been mighty for America, but it was crucial for Jersey City mayor Frank Hague. He had become a national figure in 1932 when Franklin D. Roosevelt, running for president the first time, came to campaign along the Jersey shore. Hague took everybody from Jersey City but the pigeons and lined the shore road with 120,000 citizens. Roosevelt sat in a touring car with his campaign manager, James A. Farley.

They roared in the salt air for Roosevelt. Farley cocked his head to hear what a cluster of reporters was calling out. "They want to know what you think of this," Farley said.

Roosevelt called to the reporters: "Frank Hague is my mayor."

Hague then stood in City Hall, Jersey City, and announced, "I am the law."

Hague lived in a penthouse at 2600 Hudson Boulevard. He also had a large suite in the Plaza Hotel on Fifth Avenue in Manhattan and another apartment on Park Avenue, where he was to die much later. He could reside in such places because his income from Jersey City, supplemented by his ownership of the city's numbers business, easily paid bills for the most splendid living. He did not countenance anything second class.

For Robinson's first game, Hague had 52,000 tickets printed for a ballpark that seated 24,500, their distribution being handled by ward committeemen who went from store to store, giving each owner 10 tickets, for which the owner paid on the spot. The committeemen then went to residential streets and sold homeowners 10 tickets each. All money was turned in to City Hall.

On opening day, ward leaders had all school buses packed. City workers put fresh paint on the first thirty-five rows of the grandstand, and another crew placed new sod over the entire field.

The mayor proclaimed that this was now an official holiday for all Jersey City, for schools, businesses, everyone who enjoys a baseball game. Hague said that no housewife should be in the kitchen cooking when she could be on a bus to the ball game.

As his high school was closed, Frank Borsky, fifteen, with a ticket from his father, who had a paint store on Fairmont Avenue, boarded a bus in the ninth ward for a trip to the game. He arrived to become part of a mob looking for a place to stand. The 24,500 seats had been gone for hours. The crowd was in the aisles and spilled onto the field.

The official attendance was 51,873.

At 2:30, the fans were thrilled by a marching band that came in from a right-field gate and played "Take Me Out to the Ball Game." Everyone bellowed in song.

Next, a gate in centerfield opened to reveal what appeared to be the mayor being burned at the stake. The hot sunlight exploding on the diamond stickpin in his tie enveloped Hague in a champagne-colored flame. He was a magnificent sight. Blue-gray eyes sparkled under a spanking new hat atop his bald head. He had on a dark blue double-breasted suit that was just out of the hands of a fine tailor. The crowd stilled for the national anthem. Then Hague marched across the new sod to his box seat behind first base. He greeted Branch Rickey and then sat in glory.

The game began. Soon the announcer called over the loudspeaker, "At second base for the Montreal Royals, Jackie Robinson."

The crowd shook the air. These good citizens of Jersey City were not so delirious at the sight of a black player, but all realized that Mayor Hague wanted them to appreciate Robinson, and if they did not, then one look around the premises showed police every few yards, all with official permission, even encouragement, to beat the brains out of anybody who dared to boo.

In his first time up, Robinson, who was dead nervous, grounded out. Embarrassed anger rose in him. In his second at bat, with two on, he hit a home run over the left-field fence. He then hit three singles. Two were bunts. Watching Robinson drop those bunts and tear to first base, Branch Rickey waved his hands and called out, "Andy High's Play!" It was High, the great scout, who had stressed Robinson's ability to bunt. He also stole second twice.

At day's end, Montreal won by many runs. The crowd crushed Robinson, seeking autographs; Rickey had a joyous ride back to Brooklyn; and Frank Hague walked up the steps of City Hall with the bearing of Caesar on a good day.

CHAPTER EIGHT

It is the summer of 1946 and Jackie Robinson is playing for the Montreal Royals minor league team. He hits .349 and steals forty bases. Certainly his talent will bring him to the National League next year. The state now has a new law behind him. And so the major league baseball owners decide he must be stopped.

The team owners met in Chicago and issued a report on Robinson, which read:

RACE QUESTION

The appeal of Baseball is not limited to any racial group. The Negro takes great interest in baseball and is, and always has been, among the most loyal supporters of Professional Baseball.

The American people are primarily concerned with the excellence of performance in sport rather than the color, race or creed of the performer. The history of American sport has been enriched by the performance of great Negro athletes who have attained the mythical All-American team in football; who have won world championships in boxing; and who have helped carry Americans to track-and-field victory in the Olympic games. Fifty-four professional Negro baseball players served with the Armed Forces in this war—one player was killed and several wounded in combat.

Baseball will jeopardize its leadership in professional sport if it fails to give full appreciation to the fact that the Negro player and the Negro fan are part and parcel of the game. Certain groups in this country, including political and social-minded drumbeaters, are conducting pressure campaigns in an attempt to force major league clubs to sign Negro players. Members of these groups are not primarily interested in Professional Baseball. They are not campaigning to find a better opportunity for thousands of Negro boys who want to play baseball. They are not even primarily interested in improving the lot of Negro players who are already employed. They know little about baseball—and nothing about the business end of its operation. They single out Professional Baseball for attack because it offers a good publicity medium.

The thousands of Negro boys of ability who aspire to careers in professional baseball should have a better opportunity. Every American boy, without regard to his race or his color or his creed, should have a fair chance in baseball. Jobs for half a dozen good Negro players now employed in the Negro leagues are relatively unimportant. Signing of a few Negro players for the major leagues would be a gesture—but it would contribute little or nothing towards a solution of the real problem. Let's look at the facts:

A major league baseball player must have something besides great natural ability. He must possess the technique, the coordination, the competitive attitude, and the discipline, which is usually acquired only after years of training in the minor leagues. The minor league experience of players on the major league rosters, for instance, averages 7 years. The young Negro player never has a good chance in baseball. This is the reason there are not more players who meet major league standards in the big Negro leagues.

The paper quoted Sam Lacy, of the Baltimore *Afro-American*, as saying that Negroes were "simply not good enough to make major leagues at this time." The owners were preposterous liars. They also have Lacy, who strained all his life trying to get a black into baseball, saying, "I am reluctant to say that we haven't a single man in the ranks of colored baseball who could step into the major leagues and disport himself after the fashion of a big leaguer." Sam Lacy never said such a thing. The owners knew it. The report went on:

If the major leagues and big minors of Professional Baseball raid these leagues and take their best players—the Negro leagues will eventually fold up—the investments of their club owners will be wiped out— and a lot of professional Negro players will lose their jobs. The Negroes who own and operate these clubs do not want to part with their outstanding players—no one accuses them of racial discrimination.

The Negro leagues rent their parks in many cities from clubs in Organized Baseball. Many major and minor league clubs derive substantial revenue from these rentals. (The Yankee Organization, for instance, nets nearly $100,000 a year from rentals and concessions in connection with Negro league games in Yankee Stadium in New York—and in Newark, Kansas City, and Norfolk.) Club owners in the major leagues are reluctant to give up revenues amounting to hundreds of thousands of dollars every year. They naturally want the Negro leagues to continue. They do not sign and cannot properly sign players under contracts to Negro clubs. This is not racial discrimination. It's simply respecting contracts.

There are many factors to this problem and many difficulties which will have to be solved before any satisfactory solution can be worked out. The individual action of any one Club may exert tremendous pressure upon the whole structure of Professional Baseball and could conceivably result in lessening the value of several major league franchises.

The owners' vote on this report was 15–1 in favor. Rickey was the only one against. He walked out of the meeting in Chicago in cold anger. When he got back to Brooklyn, he found he didn't have a copy of the statement. He called for one and was told that all had been destroyed, at which point he knew the owners were going to try to evade, duck, and short-circuit the law. He walked out of his office and flew to Blue Grass Field in Lexington, Kentucky, a place of sprawling horse farms and a university and the home of baseball's new commissioner, Albert B. Chandler, known as "Happy," who was in the office behind his house. Rickey sat in a leather chair.

"Rickey told me that he couldn't go ahead in face of that vote," Chandler recalled. "He said, 'I can't do it unless I have your full support.'"

"Can this man play?" Chandler recalls asking Rickey.

"He could make the major leagues today."

"Then bring him on."

Through all this time in New York, while Rickey is trying to change America, there are eight large daily newspapers. The true calling of news reporting was to reach into the sky and try to change some of the sour patches of earth beneath. It never happened. A few Southern editors stood up for blacks, and their actions were so monumental that these men are still known today—Ralph McGill of Atlanta, and Hodding Carter of Mississippi, and Harry Ashmore of Little Rock, to name the most obvious. Hugo Germino of the Durham *Herald-Sun*, Smith Barrier of the Greensboro, North Carolina, *Daily News*, and Frank Spencer of the *Winston-Salem Journal* believed that Robinson was at least a human being and wrote about him as such.

No white editor in the North became a civil rights legend because no white in the North wanted anything to do with it.

Some years later, Bob Teague, who played football at Wisconsin and therefore had an aura of fall leaves and Saturday-afternoon Big Ten games, was hired by the *New York Times* and worked quite successfully for many years. Teague was black.

Always he covered sports. Only a few subway stops away from the paper's offices was Harlem, where children were raised in poverty and went to schools that did not teach.

They were not called reporters then, they were known as baseball writers, or boxing writers, or racing writers. Those were the big jobs in the sports departments. If you covered racing you got the chance to be with the grandest of people, the Whitneys and Woodwards. The boxing writers hung around with real men, including managers who were always ready with a payoff, whether it was required or not. I covered two fights when the boxing writer was away in my time at the old Hearst paper in New York, the *Journal-American*. I am stuck in snow at three in the morning and so I take a room at the Hotel Edison. I go to the all-night drugstore at Broadway and 50th to get toothpaste and a toothbrush. From a snowbank on the corner leaps Sol Gold, a co-manager of the great middleweight champion Tony Zale. He leaps in front of me so he can pay for the toothbrush and toothpaste.

Since baseball was top in readership, its writers had the best jobs. Just hours after New Year's Day they were en route to Florida or Arizona. Someday they would fly, but back then they traveled by Pullman from city to city and stayed in top hotels and ran up so many overtime days that they never had to answer the phone or do a lick of work in the off-season. There were three major league teams in New York and writers were assigned to them permanently and for years. They regarded themselves as part of the team, as in, "We're playing Detroit tomorrow." The writers covering the Yankees were preposterously stodgy. Those with the Dodgers liked golf, for some reason. Since the Giants were owned by an alcoholic, the writers all drank heavily. One writer, Joe King, of the *World-Telegram*, wrote with Balzac's dagger in every sentence about the Giants' manager, Leo Durocher. In return, Leo went to the taxicab that took King away from the old Polo Grounds ballpark each night and left a note saying "You are a stumbling drunken bum."

In the Cincinnati Reds' old Crosley Field, two big, wonderful German women had a counter near the press box from which they served the largest sandwiches in all of baseball, and maybe sports. Surely, members of the Baseball Writers Association deserved such service, even though, because of them, there was not a black mouth to feed.

The Baseball Writers Association of America organization was a fake and a fraud, a shill as white as the Klan. The teams paid the way for the writers traveling with them, starting with spring training. They also gave the writers $8 a day meal money. Only one or two newspapers declined to be part of such a corrupt arrangement. The others were delighted to save the money.

The association was in charge of all press boxes at baseball games, and only reporters working for daily newspapers, and thus only whites, were permitted to enter. Association rules kept out reporters from the weekly papers, almost all of whom were black. There was the New York *Amsterdam News* and similar papers in Pittsburgh, Chicago, Baltimore, and elsewhere, all shut out.

In Brooklyn, the only reporter from a weekly paper admitted to the Baseball Writers Association was Jack Butler of the *Brooklyn Tablet*, the official publication of the borough's Roman Catholic Diocese. As there were perhaps fifteen black Catholics in the entire diocese, this made their weekly newspaper safe and white.

The association rules were so sinful and scandalous that even a faint voice in protest could have shattered the arrangement. But it continued to exist because the team owners allowed it. The newsmen opposed not. Everybody was silently satisfied at working in the atmosphere of a restricted country club. Comfort would be ruined by the opening of the door for even one black sports reporter. Who would sit next to him?

When the rumor of Jackie Robinson first turned real, the association polled members in each city. Someone had the notion that a strong negative reaction to Robinson by baseball writers would keep him out. It did not. In Cincinnati, there was a single vote against Robinson. Everybody assumed it had been cast by Tom Swope of the *Cincinnati Post*, an old-timer, gruff as a watchman. Swope said nothing. Of course he was far better than voting to keep some infielder from earning a living just because he has dark skin.

In New York, Jimmy Powers, the sports editor of the *Daily News*, then with a circulation of nearly three million, wrote not even one column during this time that called for making room for black players. The thought of Powers, with that immense circulation behind him, losing the clear chance to become a new and commanding figure in America causes you to wince. Oh, he lost that chance, don't worry about that. He was the most persistent and vicious of Rickey's enemies. He delighted whites who saw blacks as not just playing baseball but also taking white men's jobs in the iron workers' union.

In 1946, from June until September, Powers wrote eighty columns against Rickey.

Rickey had neither met nor even seen Powers. At an exhibition game at Yankee Stadium, Rickey told his press agent, Harold Parrott, "Tell me what he's wearing. So when I look around I'll know him." Powers wasn't there. He never went anywhere except to Madison Square Garden, where he announced the Friday-night fights on television for Gillette razors, and the mobsters who promoted the fights under the name of the International Boxing Club. Otherwise, he wrote his column and went to the golf course in Westchester.

Faced with this barrage from Powers, Rickey plunged into temporary madness himself. He and his people at 215 Montague Street put together a thirty-seven-page rebuttal. "His charges are poisonous smokescreens, personal vilification, innuendoes, colored exaggerations, half truths, untruths, flat lies," they wrote.

Rickey showed it to John Smith, who as president of Pfizer understood that you survive on remaining cool and patient and not stumbling. He told Rickey, "Your mode of refuting Powers's assertions dignifies them and adds weight to them." Smith knew that someone practicing prolonged lousiness usually winds up falling into your lap. And in this he was correct.

One day in 1949, Rickey received a copy of a letter Powers had written to somebody in his business:

I talked to the captain last night [the publisher of the *Daily News*] and he told me not to worry about latrine gossip picked up by the FBI. That if Winchell and the rest of the Jews had their way, America would be a vast concentration camp from Maine to California. There wouldn't be enough barbed wire to hold back all the decent Christians maligned by the Jews and those who run with them. In short, I was in pretty good company with him, with Col. McCormick, Joe Kennedy and several other decent family men . . . How in hell can I be termed 'pro-Nazi' simply because I don't happen to like certain crackpot politicians and Jews?

The letter brought jubilation to the Dodgers' office mail room. A guy called out, "This does it!"

"And you are doing what?" Rickey asked.

"Sending it to every newspaper in the city," the mail room guy said.

"No, you're not. You're throwing it away," Rickey said. "Nobody is to know this exists. I've never sunk low enough to do a thing like this. I never should have taken him seriously. Now we can forget him."

Rickey called John Smith at Pfizer and thanked him profusely for being right. Of course only the owner of heaven could walk completely away from a wonderful opportunity to inflict some discomfort on a rat that had been gnawing on his feet for some time. Somebody in the Brooklyn office called Powers and told him that Rickey had the letter and was holding it and would do nothing with it. Immediately, Powers looked out the *Daily News* sports department window at 42nd Street and took many deep breaths to keep his heart from stopping dead. After which he never wrote another bad word about Branch Rickey.

Rickey then—just for nothing, for he never would think of getting even—sent free passes to Dodgers games to Powers and his family. Powers promptly answered: "I appreciate your thoughtfulness very much. I too wish you a lot of luck, and if there is anything I can do for you during the season, I will be glad to do all I can do to help you."

Of the other white sports reporters in New York, none matched the bitterness of columnist Joe Williams of the *World Telegram*, a Scripps-Howard paper. He was out of Memphis, and it showed. By printing Williams's tobacco road views, the publishers showed support for them. He never quit. In 1946 Williams wrote that Rickey deliberately lost the pennant race for the Dodgers by trading second baseman Billy Herman to the Boston Braves and postponing a championship until the next year, when Robinson's arrival would make it "a Negro Triumph." Then, a few years later, when Robinson was a fixture with the Dodgers, Williams wrote, "It might help Jackie Robinson if he remembered that he came into the majors as a ballplayer, not a symbol."

Robinson caused the gravest of all fears: what if this black man makes it and then there is another one after him and soon a third and fourth and more, then what will happen to our way of life, this national pastime, if these players take everything and the whites we applauded turned out not to be so great and wound up working in Southern gas stations? And what if our fans can't stand sitting next to blacks and leave the ballparks and the game? Civilized society had to rely on outsiders who came out of alleys to call for beliefs and behaviors that were supposed to be American.

The man Rickey needed so badly was just out of his reach. His name was Dave Egan and he wrote for the *Boston Record*, a Hearst tabloid. As early as the 1930s, he wrote things like, "The kings of baseball can bay to the moon and howl to the stars but there is no way for them to shuck off the fact that theirs is a sport that is no more national than the trolley to Brookline. How can you claim to represent the nation while you exclude anybody not of white caucasian extraction?"

CHAPTER NINE

This is February of 1947, just weeks before the start of baseball season. Branch Rickey is walking into the Carlton Branch of the YMCA in Brooklyn to talk to thirty civic leaders, all men of color, about Robinson. Of the six points he had written down at the start of this grand experiment, he had achieved all but one: "the backing and thorough understanding from the Negro race, to avoid misrepresentation and abuse of the project." Now he was setting to finish the job.

He got up right away. "I'm not going to tell you what you hope to hear. Someone close to me said I didn't have the guts to tell you what I wanted to do; that I didn't have the courage to give it and that you people wouldn't be able to take it. I believe all of us here tonight have the courage. I have a ballplayer named Jackie Robinson . . . on the Montreal team . . . He may stay there . . . He may be brought to Brooklyn. But if Jackie Robinson *does* come up to the Dodgers the biggest threat to his success—the *one* enemy most likely to ruin that success—is the Negro people themselves!

"I say it as cruelly as I can to make you all realize and appreciate the weight of responsibility that is not only on me and my associates but on Negroes everywhere. For on the day Robinson enters the big league—*if* he does—every one of you will go out and form parades and welcoming committees. You'll strut. You'll wear badges. You'll have Jackie Robinson Days and Jackie Robinson Nights. You'll get drunk. You'll fight. You'll get arrested. You'll wine and dine the player until he is fat and futile. You'll symbolize his importance into a national comedy . . . and an ultimate tragedy—yes, tragedy!

"For let me tell you this. If any individual, group, or segment of Negro society uses the advancement of Jackie Robinson in baseball as a triumph of race over race, I will regret the day I ever signed him to a contract, and I will personally see that baseball is never so abused and misrepresented again!"

When he sat down it was reported that there was tremendous applause. Maybe, but that speech did not succeed with Rachel Robinson. Many years later, she said, "That speech. It was racist. I'd like to forget it."

At the start of spring training, Robinson is still with Montreal, but everybody knows this is a fake. The Dodgers were training at an old military base in Panama for an exhibition game against a team of Carribean all-stars. Most knew that Robinson was only days away. The manager, Leo Durocher, spent a day going around and telling one player after another, "Isn't it great we're going to have Robinson? He can get a pennant for us." Leo did not like the reactions. He heard a whisper that Dixie Walker was starting a petition against Robinson. Leo went to bed and thought for a long time. If these imbeciles give their petition to Rickey, he figured, they are making the thing official. It'll break this club up. I'm supposed to get World Series money this year. These fucks and their petition are going to take money out of my pocket.

He swung out of bed. "Get everybody up!"

There were two ways of addressing ballplayers at this time.

One was Rickey's indirection, verbal subterfuge, calling for a religious book, a story about Ty Cobb, anything to delay and confuse and soften the path.

Then there was Durocher's way. Right now, he stands in the big military base kitchen, with players seated on steam tables and chopping blocks. No newspaper people were present. They needed their sleep. But everybody who was there, from Durocher down, told of his speech so frequently that it became an official final score.

"I hear some of you fellas don't want to play with Robinson," he said, "and that you have a petition drawn up that you are going to sign. Well, boys, you know what you can do with that petition. You can wipe your ass with it. Mister Rickey is on his way down here and all you have to do is tell him about it. I'm sure he'll be happy to make other arrangements for you.

"I hear Dixie Walker is going to send Mister Rickey a letter asking to be traded. Just hand him the letter, Dixie, and you'll be gone. Gone! If this fellow is good enough to play on this ball club—and from what I've seen and heard, he is—he is going to play on this ball club and he is going to play for me.

"I'm the manager of this ball club and I'm interested in

one thing," he continued. "Winning. I'll play an elephant if he can do the job, and to make room for him I'll send my own brother home. So make up your mind to it. This fellow is a real great ballplayer. He's going to win pennants for us. He's going to put money in your pocket and money in mine. And here's something else to think about when you put your head back on the pillow. From everything I hear, he's only the first—ONLY THE FIRST, BOYS. There's many more coming right behind him and they have the talent and they gonna come to play. These fellows are hungry. They're good athletes and there's nowhere else they can make this kind of money. They're going to come, boys, and they're going to come scratching and diving. Unless you fellows wake up and look out, they're going to run you right out of the ballpark. So I don't want to see your petition and I don't want to hear any more about it. The meeting is over—go back to bed."

When Rickey reached Panama he had a morning meeting with Dixie Walker, which angered him plenty, and then another with Bobby Bragan, young and sullen, a reserve catcher from Fort Worth. He stood alongside Rickey with his fists clenched and his face contorted. He came from a contractor's household where he answered black workers at the back door asking for a two- or three-dollar advance on their pay.

"Are you here to tell me you do not want to play with Robinson?" Rickey asked.

"Yes."

"Then I shall accommodate you. I must have your word on one matter. It might take some time for us to effect a trade for you. Will you promise to try your best for this team until the trade is worked out?"

Flashing eyes answered. Do you think I would lay down on anyone?

Rickey said he would trade him, but he did not. Instead he put his trust in proximity. On twelve-day road trips to three and four cities, Bobby Bragan remembers today, "the most popular players, Gil Hodges, Pee Wee Reese, Duke Snider, Hal Gregg, all were at the table with Robinson in the dining car. We were outsiders. Me, Carl Furillo, Eddie Stanky, and Walker. I watched the table with Robinson. He liked what they said and they liked what he said. They all laughed. We were out of it. It did not last forever, I'll tell you that. We were starting on one trip and I was right at that table with Robinson and so was Stanky. I don't care where you're from, you're on a train trip and he was the best company and I don't want to be off by myself."

Hearing of this, Rickey said to Harold Parrot of his staff, "When they play cards, if you notice them gambling, act as if you didn't see it." He went for his cigars. With one word, one small act, proximity, he was sensing a hundred years starting to disappear.

Durocher had a temper that made the slightest confrontation suggest Verdun. Yet, no question, he was the manager Rickey believed he needed when they brought in Robinson. Leo was argumentative, unreasonable, a gambler who seemed to adore trouble and a manager loyal to the sky for his players. He didn't seem to notice Robinson's color.

"Be daring," Rickey kept calling to Robinson all through

spring training. When they got closer to the regular season, Robinson was on first base looking for a sign. Durocher was pacing up and down in the dugout, hands at his sides, and he shrugged and his hands came out palms up, and he paced on and Robinson began his dance and then took off and the stands went crazy as he stole second. Durocher's hands clapped in joy.

This was a beautiful partnership. Always, I can see Leo Durocher tying his tie in the manager's dressing room, talking about how he managed the game, talking, talking and then calling to admirer Spencer Tracy, who sat against the wall. "How's that, Spence? How did you like it?"

And Tracy ducked his head and shook it side to side. "Whewf."

"How's that, Spence?"

Durocher loved that. A soft night with a great friendly star. But nice also is dreadfully boring. Look out below! Durocher could cause turmoil just by remaining still.

This all started where I come from, in Ozone Park in Queens, on the night that Joe Moore chased his own son-in-law, a boss of the Mafia named Tommy Eboli Ryan, down 86th Street toward the El on Liberty Avenue. Joe sure did have a gun. Tommy Ryan knew that. Even old people on the block with faulty hearing knew the sound.

Joe Moore was an immense man who worked as a special cop, a square badge, at ball games, including Ebbets Field. The next entry on his résumé reads "Does get mad." He knew Rickey only by sight. Rickey sure recognized Moore. Upon happening to see Joe in full splendor, Rickey remarked, "The man is completely vulnerable to an attack if he doesn't lose weight." Lumbering down the street on this night, Joe Moore fired a couple shots into the Ozone Park night air. He missed, but nevertheless that is some brave gun. Ryan was the second head of the Mafia to come out of the neighborhood. First there was Vito Genovese, then Ryan, and following all, John Gotti. You do not become head of the Mafia by pushing strollers on Liberty Avenue.

Then Joe Moore went back to his trade, security work at stadiums. All of us in high school knew him because he broke up fights and stopped kids from running onto the field during school football games. When Durocher looked at Moore, however, he saw a great big guy who could beat everybody up; a useful individual. A fan in the upper deck behind third base, one with a voice that could reach New Jersey, was bellowing abuse that infuriated Durocher. "You thief," he hollered. And, "You're a crook, Durocher." The man's name was John Christian. He had just been discharged from the military. He lived in the East New York section of Brooklyn and was a known athlete from Thomas Jefferson High. Sitting with him was Dutch Garfinkel, from the same famous high school. Garfinkel was as good a basketball player as anybody ever saw and he became a national name at St. John's University. "He never cursed at Durocher," Garfinkel said. "With that loud voice he had, I told him that he should cut it out."

At the sixth inning, Durocher looked across the top of the Dodgers dugout and called Moore over and asked him for a favor. He asked Moore to tell John Christian that the manager of the Brooklyn Dodgers would be glad to come down under the stands and sign a lot of autographs and talk about the heckler's opinions. Christian somewhat naively said, sure.

"Don't go," Garfinkel said.

"No, I'll meet Durocher," Christian said. He was there under the stands after the sixth inning, right on time, and Joe Moore gave him his autograph. It was some clout, Christian testified in court. Then Durocher took his best shot. The claim was Joe Moore held the guy and Leo hit him. Christian went home in a daze, with a broken jaw, a banged-up face, and a realization that this was a matter for the police. Detectives were at Ebbets Field in time to arrest Moore and Durocher before they left.

Leo always bought trouble wholesale. First, there is the straight news reporting of the assault and arrest. With big pictures taken on the steps of the police station. The following day Christian and his broken jaw were on the front pages and as many pages inside as they could fill. If you sat in a barber shop, your ears were besieged with radio details of Durocher's attack. Rickey was fearful of losing the best manager he ever saw just at this critical moment. He also had great anxiety over the desperate ability of the Devil to take violence and pass it through the air to tempt others. In this matter, he worried most about Robinson's ability to follow the Life of Christ and turn the other cheek. "He is a proud man, powerful man and of great intelligence," Rickey said. "I am fearful of the amount of abuse we ask him to take. Judas Priest! What if he is inundated with the most scurrilous of remarks and regarding them as threats he is driven to defending himself one day. That is precisely what it would be, self-defense against assault. But he cannot do that. Oh, he knows he cannot. Not a raised eyebrow can be contested. Watch the trouble we have now. Leo is the only one I know of who is familiar with this much trouble to be able to assist Robinson."

When the Christian assault case was brought into magistrates court, a flotilla of lawyers arrived to defend Durocher. The judge was Samuel Leibowitz, who had been the lawyer for the Scottsboro Boys case in the South and the feared jurist for the Murder, Inc., trials in Brooklyn. The Dodgers lawyers suggested to Joe Moore that he take the weight for the good of the Dodgers. It was not advice well taken.

"You got somebody who doesn't give a fuck about you," Joe Moore said. "I don't give a fuck for anybody. I'll take everybody with me."

Rickey got up at a Rotary Club luncheon and looked at some of the players present and announced, "I apologize for the Brooklyn organization's failure to give you proper protection against some errant fan maligning our good athletes by making a false claim. The Dodgers must protect the player from receiving unfair, unconscionable abuse from the fans.

"Look at this case as we have investigated it," he went on. "The man here slipped on wet cement downstairs, and landed on his face. His jaw was broken, his medical people say. But what preceded this? Constant and complete vilification. No one rose to deflect such humiliating tirades against our defenseless players. And then fashioning a fable, a concocted set of events, yes, Judas Priest! A lie! What must come out of this unfairness is an ordinance, a local law prohibiting the abuse of players."

The lawyers scurried to have the case postponed repeatedly and it took a full year to get it settled in a cooler atmosphere. With so much time passed, it was somewhat difficult to ask twelve decent citizens to vote against their place of birth and their team. The lawyers paid Christian about $7,000 and he went away. Even Joe Moore went home.

But whenever Durocher walked off the field he headed for trouble as if it was his home address. In one instance it was. He let George Raft and a platoon of thieves use his Manhattan apartment for cards and dice that made you lose. A couple of the gamblers let out the loudest sound in sports: a sucker's holler.

One day, from Los Angeles, there arose a howl from a man who regarded himself as being married to actress Laraine Day:

LEO STEALS HOME—LARAINE'S HUBBY

Leo had been married twice before. The judge in Day's divorce case said Leo had to stop being seen with Laraine or he would rule harshly.

"I am not out in public with her," Leo told a press conference. "I'm living in her home with her."

Then he did a Durocher thing. He took Laraine to Mexico and got her a divorce. Now he went to El Paso, Texas, and married her against California law.

If there was one thing that could upset the Roman Catholic Diocese of Brooklyn, it was sex. Instead of inspiring Brooklyn youth, he is sleeping with another man's wife!

Durocher also was ordered to stay away from Memphis Engelberg, the gambler; Connie Immerman, who ran the Cotton Club for New York mobsters; and Joe Doto, aka Joe Adonis because he looked so good. Adonis was one of the great New York mobsters in a period when they were treasured for the excitement they could cause.

Durocher's sins were so much greater than homicide. His was the mortaller: sex. Leo complained that Larry MacPhail of the Yankees was with more women than he had ever known. And that nobody cared. MacPhail started a squall. The Catholics were the loudest, and in Brooklyn they had numbers. The office of the Bishop announced it was considering having the Catholic Youth Organization withdraw from the Knothole Gang because of Durocher's public immorality.

They were playing Walter O'Malley's tune. He was a heavyset, pure Irish backpatter who came out of mortgages and business loans and limited partnerships, and had attached himself to the Brooklyn Trust Company. Rickey was having trouble with the Brooklyn Catholics. He asked fellow baseball man and team co-owner O'Malley if he could keep the Catholics on his side. Sure, purred O'Malley. Instead, he went to Bishop Malloy of Brooklyn and said: "Isn't it a hideous thing to have this Durocher with his three wives and adultery being held up as an example for good Catholic youth? I truly can't understand why Rickey allows this to happen. I am distressed to talk about this, but your Father Powell is correct, I feel, in protecting the Catholic Youth Organization by keeping the children away from Dodgers games."

Of a Brooklyn morning in April 1947, Rickey had a large meeting at the Dodgers office about the season that was starting, and the farm teams, when his private phone interrupted him. He took the call and listened in silence. Then he roared, "You son of a bitch!" Nobody had heard him swear before. When he hung up, he informed Durocher, "That was the commissioner. You've been suspended from baseball for the year."

"For what?" Durocher cried.

Officially it was for gambling, but really it was for everything. Small, large. He had them crazy. What hurt Rickey most was that Durocher wouldn't be on the field when Robinson needed help.

CHAPTER TEN

Early in the morning of April 10, 1947, Branch Rickey woke up Jackie Robinson and told him to come to the Dodgers offices right away. When Robinson got there, he was given a contract to sign. He was told to report to the clubhouse at Ebbets Field, where the team was playing an afternoon exhibition game against its Montreal farm club, the last before the regular season. At the field he would find the interim manager, Clyde Sukeforth, with whom he might be somewhat familiar.

Rickey then dictated a memo to his secretary, Jane Ann Jones. He told her to make one carbon. It read:

> The Brooklyn Dodgers today purchased the contract
> of Jack Roosevelt Robinson from the Montreal Royals.
> He will report immediately.
>
> Branch Rickey

Jane Ann's nephew, a detective I knew from out on the streets, told me that Rickey took the original and put it in his inside jacket pocket. The carbon was given to Arthur Mann, an assistant. Mann brought it to the ballpark and passed it down the line in the press box during the sixth inning. Of course the paper was then lost. It wound up under the feet of one of those Phi Beta Kappas in the press box and thereafter in the dust pan of a cleaning man.

It was the great historical document of the time. Over the years, we heard that Rickey's family had the original. Or maybe it was in a desk someplace, who knew? Burt Roberts, a judge in the Bronx, and I thought that maybe if it was around in a drawer someplace, we could find it and donate it to the Brooklyn Museum or to the Library of Congress and have the satisfaction of being civic heroes and of course having a small plaque hung near the memo thanking us profusely for the donation.

I took a chance and called Rickey's daughter in Elmira, New York.

"Oh, the nicest man bought that from Daddy and donated it to the Library of Congress," she said.

"What happened?" Burt Roberts asked.

"We got thrown out at first," I said.

"Hey, nigger!"

Here is Ben Chapman, manager of the Philadelphia Phillies baseball team, standing on the top step of the dugout at Ebbets Field in Brooklyn in April of 1947.

"Hey, nigger, go back to the cotton field where you belong."

Jackie Robinson, in one of his first times to bat as a Brooklyn Dodger, walks pigeon-toed to the batter's box. His face shows nothing. He fights to keep down everything he ever believed. If hit, hit back. Can't do that now. When challenged, smack first. Can't do that, either. Insulted, call them on it, right in their faces. No good, either. I can't even turn my head to look at him, Robinson thought. If I see him, I'm not going to be able to stop myself.

Chapman had been a thoroughly forgettable outfielder and pitcher with the Dodgers and Yankees, during which time he made frequent anti-Semitic remarks. We were fighting World War II but he reserved his patriotism for home.

Upstairs, in his box suspended from the upper tier, Branch Rickey was hunched forward, kneading his hands anxiously. "Papini," Buzzie Bavasi remembered him saying. On that first day in the Dodgers offices at Montague Street, he and Robinson had read the parts of Giovanni Papini's book *Life of Christ* that inspired Robinson to accept the ideal of turning the other cheek. It is a lofty thought, and one that Robinson has promised to keep and knows that he should, but it is so immensely difficult because somebody just said he was a nigger again and his bones are raging.

In his box, Branch Rickey calls out, "What are they saying to Robinson?" Looking down, he knows the answer. A concession man selling beer behind home plate is waving to another one a few rows up and this one comes down, balancing his beer, and now the two of them stand excitedly and Rickey knows exactly what it is about and he goes down onto the field and speaks to Robinson.

"We have an agreement. That you ignore these people for three years."

"I'm supposed to let them do this to me?"

"For three years. Here you're not even here for a week."

"Do you know what it's like to have somebody doing this to you?"

"No, you do. And I can tell you precisely what you can do about it. Stand up and hit. Walk up there and listen to none of this and show them what you do with a bat."

He did nothing the first time up. Later in the game, he singled. When the Phillies kicked the ball around, he went to third, and then scored on Gene Hermanski's single. The Dodgers won, 1–0, and the pitcher, Hal Gregg, decided it wasn't so bad to have Robinson out there behind him.

The next day, Chapman got right back up on the top dugout step, chesty and cheap, and continued a career of lousiness by calling more names at Robinson.

"Hey, nigger . . ."

This time, Eddie Stanky of the Dodgers stood in front of the Phillies dugout and snarled at Chapman: "You yellowbelly. You know he can't answer you. I'd like to see you do it if he was free to fight back."

Rickey used the 1947–48 off-season for speaking. He made a speech at Wilberforce College in Ohio that was somewhat longer than a full reading of the Constitution. Wilberforce was a black school that was a part of the foundation of America. By then so was Rickey, and he made sure you knew it. The young students couldn't contain themselves. The man speaking to them had just reached out and pointed to the world and told them it was theirs. They had heard so many people talking to them and of course nothing was learned, except to reiterate that black is black. Suddenly, dramatically, they were hearing that color no longer mattered from a man who had an official license to say so. He was Branch Rickey, who had put Jackie Robinson into baseball and he was telling them that this big, new, wide-open world is theirs and get out there and take it.

"I believe that racial extractions and color hues and forms of worship become secondary to what men can do," Rickey said. "The denial of equality of opportunity to qualify for work to anyone, anywhere, any time, is un-understandable to me."

He then reported to the audience, and for the first time anywhere, that the baseball owners had tried to keep Robinson out of baseball by a 15–1 vote. In giving a meticulous account of his Robinson adventure, Rickey was often unable to overcome shyness about his vote.

A bone spur in the ankle had Jackie limping by the end of 1947. An operation during the off-season left him unable to do anything. He gained weight. Around this time, his close friend, the Reverend Karl Everette Downs, who had married Rachel and Jack, had a heart attack and was turned away by the white doctors at the hospital in Austin, Texas, and died. This drove Robinson to candy bars, which were his enemy. He put on thirty pounds at least.

At spring training in 1948, Durocher, back from his year's suspension, watched Robinson come onto the field as one would inspect livestock up for sale.

"How can he put his shoes on?" Durocher wondered. "Last year he was great. I get here and he shows up a fat cook."

Robinson had to suffer through a spring training of sweat and groans. Flop on your belly and come right off the ground and flop on the ground and come off the ground and do this again because this is a drill without end.

By season's end Robinson had been in 147 games and hit .296. Pretty good.

In 1949 Robinson exploded. He was in 156 games, had 203 hits, 16 home runs, 124 runs batted in, and hit .342. Each time he got on base, the crowd shimmered with excitement. He walked right off the bag in the pitcher's face. He danced, faked, started, stopped, and then ran. His slide was pure form. He stole 37 bases in that season. "He prepared himself for this," Rickey said, extolling his sliding pit exercises in spring training. That season, Robinson was named the Most Valuable Player, which was an understatement.

Behind him, applauding, crying compliments, was Rickey. He did a great thing in American life, yet he was mortal. He soon came to illustrate perfectly the mutual envy of politicians and businessmen. The politician cannot restrain himself from taking his brilliance into the world of business. Before long, he is on a breadline. The businessman is sure that he can run the world, and given a chance he is out there on the public stage. Soon the people are ready to garrote him. The wise shoemaker sticks to his trade and maintains a mouth filled with nails. That was not to be Rickey or Robinson.

This particular thing began on April 19, 1949, when Paul Robeson, the magnificent singer and actor, speaking in Paris, said, "It is unthinkable that American Negroes would go to war on behalf of those who have oppressed us for generations against a country which in one generation has raised our people to full human dignity."

"They won't fight for their country?" In the halls of Congress, that cry was heard, most loudly in the House Un-American Activities Committee, which was sending out telegrams asking public figures to appear at a special hearing on Robeson's speech. An early wire went to Robinson.

Rickey could not wait to send Robinson to testify about Robeson's speech. "I was in France in World War I," Rickey said. "There were men of color dead. I believe they fought for their country. Jackie Robinson was in uniform. What does this man Robeson know about such things?" At a meeting, Buzzie Bavasi and nine others in the Dodgers office were against Robinson testifying. They thought he would show too much anger. Then Rickey cast his vote, which weighed more than all the others.

Rickey sat at his desk and began writing a statement for Robinson to give before Congress. He had everybody in the room do the same. Rickey ended up with many drafts but he suspected that something was wrong with all of them. He was right: white men were trying to write the passion of a black man. He asked Lester Blackwell Granger of the Urban League to lend a hand. They sat in Rickey's dining room and worked on a script that seemed fine and suddenly Robinson was talking about it to a United Press reporter.

"I'll fight any aggressor," Robinson said. "Any aggressor as well as the Russians . . . I've been treated very well. I'll fight anyone who tries to take away my American heritage. I want to fight for my child's right to live in this country and for any other child's."

A few days later, on July 18, 1949, Robinson and his wife, Rachel, came into a congressional hearing room that was crowded and tense. He read his script, which ended with him saying, "We can win our fight without the Communists, and we don't want their help."

Rushing then from Congress to Ebbets Field, he drew a walk in the sixth inning and immediately, rocking back and forth, taunting, he stole second. The catcher threw wild trying to stop him. He flew to third. Now he prowled down the base line. The Cubs pitcher watched him over and over. Robinson was gone in the middle of a look.

In the eighth inning he hit a triple, and the instant he got his foot on the bag off it came and he started down that line and in the confusion the pitcher balked and Robinson walked home.

"He thrilled his country all day and saved the last great thrill for Brooklyn at night," Rickey said after the game.

Robinson started in six All-Star games. He played in his first World Series in 1952 and in game one hit a home run against Allie Reynolds of the Yankees. By then he was no longer unique in baseball. Don Newcombe, the black pitcher Clyde Sukeforth saw in the rain, was on the mound for the Dodgers. Soon the Dodgers had three blacks, and the team won six pennants, a World Series, and finished second three times and third once. Robinson was Rookie of the Year, National League Batting Champion, and Most Valuable Player. Roy Campanella was voted Most Valuable three years. Don Newcombe was Rookie of the Year and Most Valuable once.

Rickey kept one aspect of Brooklyn baseball history on a shelf well out of reach. That was the Daffiness Boys reputation that so many loved because it was real. Rickey wanted to win

116

games not laughter. Now came through the door a Queens County high school graduate, William Loes, who brought back the past. Because he could pitch, Rickey signed him. Because he made everybody laugh and feel better, Loes is remembered today as a great Rickey success.

Rickey's best-known afternoon in Brooklyn came when Loes was a high school prospect from the Astoria neighborhood in Queens when he arrived in Brooklyn one afternoon with his father and George Douris, who had been the official scorer for Loes's no-hitters with Bryant High School. They went to lunch with Rickey, which made Loes's father nervous about the check. "Don't worry," Douris said. He couldn't pay either.

Rickey asked Loes if he had a girlfriend. Billy took this as a question of his manhood. "I don't care about girlfriends. I want to know how much money you're going to pay me," Billy said.

He was twenty and an afternoon out of a high school hallway and he was going right against the famous Branch Rickey. Of course this was the act of a daffy boy. So daffy he walked out with a $21,000 bonus; in that year and in Astoria, in Queens, it was most wonderful money.

In the old and famous baseball field in Brooklyn, Ebbets Field, there were two decks behind home plate and on October afternoons there were moments when the sun came between the two decks and blazed in the eyes of a pitcher. Which was Billy Loes's occupation for the then Brooklyn Dodgers, now in Los Angeles.

He was on that mound and open to those sunrays in the 1952 World Series against the Yankees. That year, he was back from army service and won thirteen games, pitching four shutouts and with an earned run average of 2.69. In his four best years for the Dodgers he won fifty games. That was hardly humorous for batters. Everybody else made Loes daffy.

The night before the 1952 World Series, Loes predicted the Yankees would win in seven games. In the sixth game, the baseball slipped out of his hand while he was standing on the rubber. That error moved a runner up. "Too much spit," he said. Then Vic Raschi, the Yankees' pitcher, hit a grounder that Loes bent to get but couldn't see. It slapped off his leg and caromed into right field. A run scored.

"I lost it in the sun," Loes said. He became the first player ever to lose a ground ball in the sun.

Everybody loved it. The celebrations over this also missed a small point: the sun did come through the stands in cruel rays every October, and a fine pitcher like Carl Erskine noted, "The fact is, if you ever pitched in Ebbets Field you know that's possible in October with a ball that takes a bounce."

Billy died at eighty in Tucson, Arizona. He left a smile that always goes with somebody looking him up and reading again his so highly sensible reason for it all: "Go on and write what you want about me and say I said it. You've been doing it right along anyway."

Though Durocher was back in the dugout, by July 1948 things were going badly. When the Dodgers lost six games in a row, Rickey, in the hospital with a urinary infection, sent somebody to the clubhouse to ask his manager to quit. Leo refused.

Then there was rueful rumbling from the Polo Grounds, where the sainted Mel Ott, the Giants manager, was on his way out. Rickey and Horace Stoneham of the Giants talked. "I need a manager," Stoneham said.

"Would Durocher do?" Rickey asked.

"I'll have somebody over to sign papers in an hour," Stoneham said.

The Brooklyn and Giants fans, who had been taught to hate for so long, were stunned and betrayed. The newspapers treated it like Pearl Harbor.

Eventually, Walter O'Malley saw a way to steal an entire baseball team. He became the best friend in the whole world to John Smith of Pfizer. O'Malley was bad-mouthing Rickey and talking with John Smith and George V. McLaughlin about expenses, Rickey's salary, and his inability to handle Durocher, and, oh, yes, he is a great baseball man and he is in such knots over this Robinson that we best look after running the business of the Dodgers.

O'Malley went from being a commercial lawyer working for the Dodgers' owners to someone who sat at games alongside Rickey and noisily wrangled with him. Rickey owned 25 percent of the Dodgers. In time, O'Malley also owned that amount. John Smith of Pfizer had another 25 percent as did the Brooklyn Trust Company.

Then John Smith died and his widow put their Dodgers stock in O'Malley's hands. He now controlled half the team. The Dodgers were in the kind of pennant race that makes baseball. However, there was money to be grabbed. Rickey's contract was up at the end of the year and O'Malley wouldn't give him an answer about renewing his contract as general manager.

"I'm going to walk out of here with a million dollars," Rickey announced.

"So walk," O'Malley said.

Rickey made it as far as Pittsburgh. This is a sad day for Brooklyn, George V. McLaughlin said. He happened to be at his job when he said this, and there is no crying inside a bank vault.

In Brooklyn, Rickey left behind one person who had almost always stood up for him. Years later, Jackie Robinson's widow, Rachel, as regal as anybody we've had in the city, stands in the moist night air of Coney Island while politicians and reporters and old fans crowd around a statue that showed Pee Wee Reese, the great Dodgers shortstop and still a favorite, with his arm around Robinson's shoulder. It depicted the moment in a game against the Cincinnati team when mental illness roared out of the dugout and from the grandstand and Reese in response walked over to Robinson and put an arm on Jackie's shoulder. The sports writers felt it was a great American moment. Now, on this morning dedicating the statue, trying to keep Brooklyn's baseball past alive, although the team had left for California almost fifty years before, Rachel Robinson appeared at Coney Island. She looked at the statue and recalled to herself vividly the actual scene of years before.

"This is so wonderful, you must be thrilled," Marty Markowitz, the Brooklyn borough president, said.

"Yes, it is," Rachel Robinson said.

She hated it: If there was one thing she and her husband despised, it was being patronized by whites. The pat on the shoulder by Reese was viewed as a wonderful thing, as if to say, *See, we like you.* That pat, that gesture, came only once, though. The true record of the years of Pee Wee Reese and Robinson is contained in a photo of the two walking off the field side by side after an inning. They were looking down, ballplayers going to the dugout. Reese's white left hand was only inches away from Robinson's black right hand, but neither of them noticed.

CHAPTER ELEVEN

Satchel Paige needed no monument. He needed cash. Bill Veeck knew that.

Paige was out of Mobile, Alabama, with no birth certificate to indicate his age, which on the occasion we mention here, in 1947, could have been about fifty. His schooling in Mobile was Reform School. This still is Mobile's shame, for he was a genius at American-language usage: "Don't look back. Somethin' might be gainin' on you."

He gave you three innings for your money, did Satchel, and you would have to thank him forever for giving you, a mere mortal, that much. You only had to say it once, that Satchel Paige would be pitching on Wednesday night at Dexter Park in Queens, New York. The place could hold 15,400 and it was packed by 6:00 for a 7:05 game. At 6:30 all players had finished their pregame warm-ups. There was no Paige. Max Rosner, the owner, now was at the front gate. He was fretting a little. No Paige. Then Rosner's hands started to shake. Still no Paige. Rosner soon was walking in a tight circle. At 6:40 a limousine pulled up and the great Paige got out. A valet carried his uniform. He walked straight to the dugout, where he changed. Satchel went out to the mound, threw a couple of warm-up pitches, and then was ready. He showed the crowd everything. His most famous hesitation pitch, with a great, big windup for a fastball that people could barely see, much less hit. He had a name for every pitch. Bee ball, jump ball, trouble ball. Dizzy Dean said, "If Satch and I were pitching in the same team, we'd clinch the pennant by the Fourth of July and go fishing until World Series time."

Paige usually would reach a point where he turned and instructed his outfielders to sit while he blew his fastball past batters. After this performance he left the field, stopped at the office to collect his fee, then got into his limousine for a ride to a later paid appearance or anyplace with a ballpark close enough to reach.

Bill Veeck, who employed Paige when he owned the Cleveland Indians back in the 1940s, called me one day in 1968 about him.

He said that Paige could not collect any pension money because he was thirty days short of having enough time on a major league team to qualify. Veeck thought this was a felony. He wanted me to call Tommy Reynolds, who owned the Atlanta Braves, and tell him he had a moral obligation to hire the pitcher as a coach for thirty days so he'd be eligible. Did he need the money? Whatever Paige had made lasted as long as a puddle in the sun.

Jack O'Neill happened to be around on the day Veeck called. O'Neill had hit .321 for Little Rock in the Southern Association and just missed coming up to the Red Sox. Finishing with the Bushwicks, he batted several times against Paige.

"How good was he, anyway?" I asked O'Neill.

"Pretty good."

"Like how good?"

124

"Like Walter Johnson."

"He's pretty old to bring in," I said.

"You stole the start of his life. Maybe you took thirty years off him because he was black."

Paige at this time was somewhere between age sixty-nine and seventy-five. I called Reynolds, who at the moment was at the bar of the Pump Room in Chicago. I caught him with a few drinks in him and he was enthusiastic about Paige. I told him he should do the right thing and hire the old pitcher.

A couple days later he called and said that the Braves players and coaches were afraid that Paige could drop dead hitting fungoes. If he was going to be a coach, then he would have to work a little—pitch some batting practice, maybe catch somebody warming up in the bullpen, work with base runners, just enough activity. Nobody knew exactly how old Paige was, and he was not exactly forthcoming on the matter. Birth certificates were not fashionable in his time. But he had to be the oldest person on a major league roster outside maybe some ancient manager.

Reynolds hired him anyway and Paige survived through the season and got his pension. One Saturday at Shea Stadium, I took my twin boys and we stood in the tunnel under the stands and here comes Paige out of the Atlanta dressing room. He had his valet behind him, carrying a big boom box. Paige was going out to the Atlanta bullpen and he wanted music.

He came walking past us without as much as a nod.

"Hey!" I said. "You don't know me?"

"I see you," Paige said.

Royalty walked on, trailed by valet and boom box.

CHAPTER TWELVE

Jackie Robinson's hour was approaching. He was miserable with diabetes. Rickey, who had made his life, was gone to Pittsburgh.

In 1956, at thirty-seven, he was in only 117 games, with 43 runs batted in, and hit .275. In the Dodgers office they looked around: what is out there that we could get for him? The Giants had a pitcher, Dick Littlefield. Would they trade him for Robinson? The Giants owner, Stoneham, asked Robinson if he was going to play in 1957. Jackie said he would let him know later. That was a lie. He had already made an agreement with Tim Cohane of *Look* magazine to announce his retirement first in the magazine. Certainly for money. *Look* was a big, slick bi-weekly that would be the first of so many to disappear. The magazine commerce would remain a secret until surfacing as a big exclusive news story after the trade was announced. Robinson quit. He came out looking like a loyal Dodger for life.

My last memory of Robinson on the field was years earlier, him looking dazed and walking toward the clubhouse right after Bobby Thomson hit the home run to give the Giants the pennant in 1951.

Branch Rickey was a country boy from birth but he lived his career in St. Louis, Cincinnati, Pittsburgh, New York. His time in those cities was spent mostly in ballparks and offices, though. He was not much for movies or theaters or nightclubs or restaurants. His lovely granddaughter Christine, a college student, signed a contract with the Conover Model Agency in Manhattan and spent the summer there in search of bookings. Rickey was comfortable with that. She performed in public, much as his athletes did. Christine stayed at the Barbizon Hotel for Women on Lexington Avenue, which was the closest thing the city had to a young woman's chaperoned residence.

Grandfather Branch agreed with this arrangement. But his rule for her in New York was that she not go out with anyone to whom she had not been properly introduced.

One day the girl's mother called Rickey to inform him that Christine had just telephoned her, excitedly, to report that she had been properly introduced to a man who owned vending machines for a living, and he took her to a place called Jilly's Bar on 52nd Street, and it was a nice bar, a lovely bar, a wonderful bar, and they all knew her slot machine king and she met Jilly, and Jilly—you wouldn't believe it!—walked her over to the end of the bar and introduced her to *his* great friend, Frank Sinatra, who was there with his own great big bodyguard.

Rickey was gasping on the phone.

Jilly later reported to all in his joint, "Frank had to use the men's room so he told the gorilla, 'Watch her with your life. If anything happens to her, they'll reopen Alcatraz for me.'"

Rickey got Christine on the phone. "You are a beautiful flower. You have a lovely garden for your life. And you go into it and find weeds." Only her most heartfelt pleading allowed her to remain in the city and the model business until school started again in the fall.

Then Rickey was gone from Brooklyn, first back to St. Louis, which was no good for him anymore, and to Pittsburgh, which was not much better. So he sat home and watched television and went to meetings.

Rickey sits in retirement in his splendid house in Fox Chapel, outside of Pittsburgh, and watches the Pirates and the New York Yankees in the first game of the 1960 World Series. They play just down the road, at Forbes Field. In his last job in baseball, Rickey had put this Pittsburgh team together. The Pirates had a 6–2 lead going into the eighth inning. Here was Roberto Clemente, as good a player as you could ever find, and Dick Groat, Bill Virdon, Bob Skinner, and Bill Mazeroski, who was the last player Rickey scouted, and that's where it all ended, all fifty years or so of running big-league baseball teams.

Rickey's other priceless find for the Pirates, Elroy Face, just about invented relief pitching. Through his years, Rickey always said that he didn't think much of relievers. In Pittsburgh, he left Elroy Face sitting on the bullpen bench, holding a pitcher of ice water while he waited for the fire bell to ring. He is the first major leaguer to save 20 games more than once. At this moment he waits for his first chance to save a World Series game. The word "save" is what it says: the relief pitcher comes into the game with his team ahead but shaky and the other team is supposed to have a

129

shot and Elroy gets out there and calmly shatters opposing hearts by removing the bat from the hands of anybody who comes up.

He had a new pitch that year. Branch Rickey had made finding it a condition of his employment. Elroy was with the Pirates' New Orleans farm team in spring training at Fort Myers, Florida, listening to Rickey, whose sunhat was pulled down to these eyes that sparkled with excitement. Rickey, an old catcher, could talk incessantly about grips. "A fastball and a curve isn't enough," he said. "You need something, a change. To put indecision into a batter. 'What is coming now?' Put a question in the hitter's mind, to bother the timing, to raise doubt." Rickey said that Joe Page, the old Yankee relief pitcher, was around the camps looking for a job. Page was throwing an obscure pitch, a forkball. Face heard this, too. In Florida, he saw Page's hand, fingers spread wide, and watched the pitch.

That season, Elroy tried a forkball at New Orleans. The first thing he had to do was remind his forefinger and middle finger to make room for the ball. He was born with the space. Others had to work for a year to teach the fingers to spread. Even young fingers groan. The forkball was held between the two fingers without touching the seam. He threw it with a fastball motion, but the ball came out as a change of speed and right in front of the plate it dived. One way this time, another way the next. If you never saw the pitch before, and only a few had, it gave trouble to the eyes.

In spring of 1959, Rickey said to him, "I hear you have a new pitch." Face was throwing and Rickey was in the box behind the plate at Fort Pierce. His forehead was pressed against the netting. Face threw. Fastball. Well, we know he can do that. He watched Face's curve. All right. See if he has another. The forkball came in. Dropped like a stone. Again, Face threw his forkball. It dropped in another direction. Marvelous. This boy did not sit around for the full year. He worked!

In 1959 Elroy won 18 games and lost 1. These were huge days in his life and he tied them all to Rickey. When he married his fiancée, June, in her family home at McKees Rocks, he grabbed her hand during the reception and took her out to the car for a quick drive to the Pirates office at Forbes Field. It was during the All-Star break. He walked into Rickey's office with his new wife. Rickey was elated. He believed that all his players should be married. It grounded them. When Elroy said they had been married in a Catholic church, he was even happier. Rickey loved religions. A long time ago, in 1906, he promised his girlfriend, Jane Moulton, that he would marry her if he had a successful year and they would know that by June. She wanted the marriage, but wouldn't have minded if he dropped baseball. She was a merchant's daughter and was not quite delirious over these uneducated farm boys and gas station attendants. By June, Rickey was catching in the major leagues and he made good on his promise. He married Jane in 1906 in a Methodist ceremony. They were married for over fifty years.

Elroy Face later became the first person anybody in the Pirates ever saw in a Pittsburgh divorce court.

Right here in the World Series clutch, it is the eighth inning and Pittsburgh is ahead, 6–2. The first Yankee batter is on base. That's when the phone rang in the bullpen. Face was up, removing his jacket. Of course the call is for him. His first warm-up pitch to the bullpen catcher Bob Oldis is the forkball. It performs.

A batter later, Face is on the mound, and Mickey Mantle steps in. He is batting left-handed against the righty Face. He starts swishing that bat. Elroy throws his slider. He likes this pitch in a sun-shadow hour. His slider is a ripple in the light, going sideways about six inches and a little down, coming in fast in the shadow on the left-handed batter. Strike one. The next pitch is another strike. Then, at last, Elroy throws his forkball. Mantle looks for it but it escapes his eyes and dives to his knees. Mantle is furious. He is a great competitor and he is walking off with the bat on his shoulder.

It was the first of three saved World Series games by Face. Rickey watched this on television. He had started the year with great energy and plans to start a third major league. But then two heart attacks left him watching from an easy chair.

In the last inning of the seventh game of the Series, Bill Mazeroski was the lead-off man for the Pirates. The score was 9–9. Mazeroski had been a second baseman for Hollywood in the Pacific Coast League. Rickey was enthralled with Mazeroski's fast hands. They came from growing up with a coal miner father who had lost a foot in the mines and sat each day in a bare living room and rolled a baseball across a linoleum floor to his kid. Through so many hours each day, the boy bent and scooped and leaped to get his father's throws. All you had to do was mention Mazeroski's name to bring tears to Branch Rickey's eyes.

Ralph Terry, the Yankee pitcher, threw. Mazeroski looked. He did not look at the second pitch. He hit it over the left-field fence for the game and the championship and Branch Rickey sat home and watched Mazeroski's joyous gallop around the bases.

Go back a few years, to 1951, when Eddie McCarrick, a scout who had always worked for Rickey, brought a contract for the Pittsburgh Pirates minor leagues to a young ballplayer and college student, Mario Cuomo of South Jamaica, Queens, and St. John's University. The contract said Cuomo was to get $2,000 for signing. Nowhere did it say he had to do anything more than sign the paper to receive the $2,000.

His father, Andrea, stood behind the counter of the grocery store under the apartment where they lived, on the corner of 150th Street and 97th Avenue, and looked at the unfamiliar document. He was from the hills outside Naples and found English at least unfamiliar.

"Baseball?" he said.

"Yes, Pa."

"No, you finish school."

"But I can finish school and still do the baseball."

"No."

"I get two thousand dollars and I don't even have to play."

Still the father was doubtful. There then arrived a letter from Branch Rickey saying that he wanted Mario to finish college, for it would help him and the Pittsburgh Pirates system. An educated ballplayer is best, he said.

Andrea Cuomo seemed impressed with the letter. He

waited until Mario was not in the store. He then walked around to a neighborhood lawyer who spoke Italian and had him inspect the letter and the contract. The lawyer said both were all right.

On the Easter vacation break from St. John's, Cuomo went to Deland, Florida, the Pirates minor league camp, and was placed with the Brunswick, Georgia, Class D team. He was in the batting cage, trying to hit balls coming out of a fractured pitching machine. One was too high, the next in the dirt, the third perhaps hittable. The balls were scuffed. Then an old guy came into the cage. He wore khaki pants, a T-shirt, and no baseball spikes. He didn't need a uniform or much of anything else, just a bat. He was George Sisler, and when he played, he hit .400.

Cuomo had trouble with an inside pitch and Sisler said quietly, "Don't fight it." The machine threw inside and Sisler stepped back and hit the ball hard. "Now for an outside pitch," Cuomo remembers him saying, "just lean over." An outside pitch came and Sisler hit it as hard as he had the inside pitch.

Cuomo was watching him closely. Sisler had a set of eyes and a pair of hands that worked as one. A freak, Mario decided.

Chasing flies in the outfield, Cuomo put whatever he had into every pursuit and wound up with a charley horse. He was told that Rickey wanted to see him. Mario walked up to the house that was the Pirates camp headquarters. Sitting on the porch was Rickey. "He asked me about my leg and then he said you need patience. You don't run wild on the first day. Then he told me that there was a grandfather bull and his grandson on top of a hill looking at a herd of cows. The grandson said, 'Let's run down and spear one.' The grandfather said, 'Why run? Let's take our time, walk easily and spear them all.' I remember being surprised he would tell a story like that. You know, everybody in the camp received a subscription to *Guideposts*. That was a religious magazine. I was still getting it at home long after I was out of baseball.

"Rickey said he wanted to talk to me because I was going to finish college. I remember him telling me, 'You're fortunate. You have something that a lot of others can't have. Stay with your education. You can try baseball for a while and then you'll have the college helping you for the rest of your life.'"

CHAPTER THIRTEEN

There was another contest in those late years to which Branch Rickey paid attention. He thought it important that Richard Nixon sweep past Kennedy in the 1960 election. He was sure his judgment was infallible. To Rickey, the campaign between Nixon and the dreaded Kennedys looked like the final struggle. He saw the end of decades of Republican principles if his man lost, so he put in a thousand phone calls squalling about the Kennedys. One of those calls went to Jackie Robinson and, of course, Robinson listened. By then he was an executive with Chock Full o'Nuts, the fastfood chain, and this had to cause his natural resentments to rise. If this was the best he could find, a job in a company with black help that he was hired to impress, he could barely tolerate it. This was a figure known all over the world, a man with a fine mind, and they had him with countermen. In a letter to a friend, magazine editor Ray Robinson, Jackie wrote, "I feel as strongly in favor of Nixon's principles, ethics and intellectual honesty. Would you have me support a Kennedy who met with one of the worst segregationists in private and then this man, the governor of Alabama, comes out with strong support for Senator Kennedy?"

In his first hours in America, Barack Obama, Sr., made it a few feet out of the airport before the sight took his breath away. He was here to study at the University of Hawaii, whose courses appealed to him, as did the vision of a blessed Hawaiian sun. Studying in Honolulu, he brought a strong thirst. If he could have stayed away from bars, perhaps he wouldn't have missed his son's big day at the White House.

In 1960, one year after Obama arrived at the university, the major Kenyan politician Tom Mboya had 250 more American college scholarships for his Kenyan students, all of whom were to be admitted to big schools that would change their lives. Mboya had sent a telegram to members of the Senate Foreign Relations Committee, one of whom was John F. Kennedy of Massachusetts, who was starting his campaign for the presidency. A telegram also went to his eventual opponent, Vice President Richard M. Nixon, who was delighted at the notion of Kenyans on his side to impress the black vote. Call State and tell them what I want, he told his staff. Why should he, the vice president, lower himself to ask a State Department bureaucrat to fly 250 Kenyans here so they can go to great colleges? The answer is, he should have done just that. The bureaucrats turned Nixon's office down, giving clout a terrible name.

At this time, Branch Rickey was living in Pittsburgh, retired. A true Republican, he made many phone calls to Jackie Robinson, also retired, to complain about Mboya's tactic. He railed, "Kennedy will try to steal home immediately!"

Robinson agreed. He wrote bitterly against Jack Kennedy in a column for the *New York Post*. After that, he called

Senator Hugh Scott, the Republican from Pennsylvania, who came on the Senate floor to attack the Kennedys for going around the law and paying privately to bring in the Kenyan students.

Joseph P. Kennedy was on the porch of his house in Hyannis Port, Massachusetts, with three of his sons, Jack and Robert and Edward, all of whom thought it would be a smart campaign move to fly the 250 students here from Kenya. Jack Kennedy asked his father if they could pay the airfare out of the Joseph P. Kennedy, Jr. Foundation.

"When will they be at the airport in Kenya?" the father asked.

On a glorious day in the summer of 1960, Tom Mboya stood on a lawn with the Kennedys, and the Cape Cod water glistened alongside the family homes, as they spoke of a beautiful future for young blacks from Kenya's raw poverty. The airlift brought 250 young Africans to America. Rickey's team lost the election.

One afternoon, Bob Prince, the announcer for the Pittsburgh Pirates, visited Rickey at Fox Chapel. Rickey was showing him styles of bird hunting. He had his grandson, Branch III, bring out his favorite shotgun plus one for Prince. They went behind the house and young Branch scaled clay pigeons for Prince. Rickey instructed him and Prince fired.

Prince knew nothing about guns, which he revealed by blasting the air for twenty straight misses. "Let me show you," Rickey said. The grandson handed his grandfather his favorite shotgun, but in handing it over, the gun went off. It was barrel down, so only blew up the earth between

Rickey's feet. The boy remembers that his grandfather never mentioned the incident. "He wouldn't let me feel guilty about anything," the grandson said.

The record of his last days shows that there were few invitations that he turned down.

An old program from a dinner at the Daniel Boone Hotel in Columbia, Missouri, on November 13, 1965, lists Branch Rickey as speaker.

He gets there after attending the seventh game of the World Series, in Minneapolis, in which Sandy Koufax of the Los Angeles Dodgers threw a two-hit shutout. Nobody could see his pitches. It was a mixed thrill for Rickey. Koufax came out of an Ice Cream League on Flatbush Avenue, blocks from Ebbets Field, but Rickey wasn't in Brooklyn to sign him.

When he got to St. Louis, Rickey was stricken with a high fever and the hospital couldn't figure out its source. Rickey demanded his release. He had in his pocket an invitation to his induction into the Missouri Sports Hall of Fame at the Daniel Boone Hotel. Nobody wanted him to go, but he did. They arrived to sit in the wind and cold at the Missouri-Oklahoma football game. He sat in distress under a blanket. Missouri won. Back in his hotel, Rickey slept. Then he got up and went to speak at the dinner. He was sure he couldn't speak two minutes. He did somewhat better. All the time his chest was telling him that it was the bottom of the ninth.

"In football they call it guts. Courage, we call it in literature," he said from the podium. "Is there a difference between them? . . . I'll call it moral courage, and I'll give you two illustrations of it.

"There was a fellow on my team in years gone, Jim Bottomley. He had courage, he had that sort of thing that when you come to the testing point, it never occurred to him whether he had it or didn't have it.

"When the game was in the eighth inning and the score was a tie, he came to bat and he got a base on balls. A fellow named Hornsby was the batsman and the question was, with a pitcher who couldn't hold runners on base, whether to let this base runner loose.

"It so happened that the day before the game began, Burt Shotton, who was the captain of our team at that time, came up to me and said, 'Do you think Jim can play today with his bad hip? Have you seen it?'

"I said, 'No, I haven't seen it today, although I did a couple of days ago.' He had a big slider, they call it, on the right hip.

"Bottomley dressed and I said to the captain, 'If he doesn't object, if he takes fielding practice, let him play.'

"Bottomley took fielding practice and he did play. And there he stood on first base in the eighth inning with the score tied and Hornsby up.

"I had a little lecture that morning—I had morning meetings always about forty minutes long, every day for several years—and I had talked on paying the price, this thing of having some objectives on which there is no price tag. You either want it or you don't want it. You either want it so bad that it doesn't matter what the price is, you don't care what it is. The question is whether you can pay it.

"I did flash the sign to Bottomley and cut him loose to let him run if he wanted to . . . I saw him slide into second base, I saw the umpire motion him safe, a *very* close play. I saw him stand up and pull his pants away from his injured hip three or four times. I thought, That dumb fellow, he could have gone the other way, he need not have made the slide on that hip.

"The game was over. Hornsby singled. Bottomley scored. We won the game, 3–2, and I went into the dressing room.

"I said, 'Jim, why in the name of common sense didn't you slide to the left and away from that hip?'

"He just looked up at me with the most innocent stare in the world and said, 'Why, Mr. Rickey'—he always called me Mr. Rickey—'didn't you see where Maranville was standing?'

"Maranville was the opposing shortstop standing on the inside of the bag to take the throw. Bottomley had to go the other way to elude the tag. It never occurred to him to think anything about prices for anything . . .

"For the other side of it, I will use an illustration from the Bible. I don't want somebody to say I'm an old molly-coddler or anything. It just happens that this chap I'm telling you about, in my judgment, had the greatest amount of courage as any man in the Bible, more than David, Samson, or Paul. Taken by and large, he was a little fellow. I don't think he could have been over five feet tall. Wealthy, he had embossed shirts and custom-made suits. He was dressed better than anyone around Jericho . . . He was a tax gatherer . . . hated by most people . . .

"I don't believe I'm going to be able to speak any longer."

He stepped back from the podium and collapsed and fell into a coma. Branch Rickey died on December 9, 1965, a few days short of his eighty-fourth birthday. His funeral was held at the Grace Methodist Church in St. Louis. Jackie Robinson and Bobby Bragan found themselves in the back of the church. Bragan said, "Come on." He and Robinson walked down to the second pew together and took a seat.

EPILOGUE

On those Brooklyn nights, her feet remembered, Jackie Robinson ran the ballpark into bedlam. Marie F. Lewis, New York City election official and boss poll watcher, swayed from one foot to the other in the crowded polling place on the first floor of the Jackie Robinson elementary school in Brooklyn.

She was mimicking Robinson tantalizing the pitchers when he was on base.

She was a short woman with glasses and wearing a gray truck driver's cap and a blue sweater. It was early November 2008, Election Night.

"My aunt took me to Ladies Night. I don't remember nothin' but this."

She continued swaying from foot to foot. "Now you see me. Next, whooosh! I'm gone. Stealin' the base on you."

Ebbets Field was a baseball park right across the street. Now it is a high, gloomy housing project whose ground floor bears signs that read "No Ball Playing."

On this night people came across the narrow street, Sullivan Place, and into the Robinson school to vote for president of the United States. Ms. Lewis was doing her duty, watching her polls. On Election Day she usually has three hundred voters at her booth. So far today two thousand have voted here and there are hours to go. She is here until closing.

Ms. Marie Lewis sees something that stops her swaying and she walks up to this big, sullen kid with a Yankees baseball cap pulled down over his eyes. He had just tried to walk into a booth and the poll watcher wouldn't let him in.

Ms. Lewis advanced on him, her face right into his, her syntax meticulous Central Brooklyn.

"You lookin' at *jail time*."

Then came James Clark, forty-seven, in the district for eighteen years, a food service manager at a big law firm in Manhattan. And a guy carrying packages from a supermarket who said he came here from Jamaica in 1965; another who said he was from Virginia fifty-five years ago; and I am asking if anybody else here remembers Jackie Robinson playing across the street, and then there was sudden noise and I don't know precisely what time it was, but the polls were closed and somewhere a television showed Barack Obama and a whoop ran through the corridor of the Jackie Robinson elementary school and the election workers were kissing and Ms. Marie Lewis was swaying and swaggering, her feet remembering the start of the long march that got us here.

Bibliography

Barber, Red. *1947: When All Hell Broke Loose in Baseball*. Garden City, NY: Doubleday, 1982. Reprint, New York: Da Capo, 1984.

Durocher, Leo, with Ed Linn. *Nice Guys Finish Last*. New York: Simon and Schuster, 1975.

Long, Michael G., ed. *First Class Citizenship: The Civil Rights Letters of Jackie Robinson*. New York: Times Books, 2007.

Lowenfish, Lee. *Branch Rickey: Baseball's Ferocious Gentleman*. Lincoln: University of Nebraska Press, 2007.

Mann, Arthur. *Branch Rickey: American in Action*. Cambridge, MA: Riverside Press, 1957.

Polner, Murray. *Branch Rickey: A Biography*. New York: Atheneum, 1982.

Rampersad, Arnold. *Jackie Robinson: A Biography*. New York: Knopf, 1997.

Robinson, Jackie, with Alfred Duckett. *I Never Had It Made: An Autobiography*. 1972. Reprint, New York: HarperCollins, 1995.

Robinson, Rachel, with Lee Daniels. *Jackie Robinson: An Intimate Portrait*. New York: Abrams, 1996.

Tygiel, Jules. *Baseball's Great Experiment: Jackie Robinson and His Legacy*. New York: Oxford University Press, 1983.